Understand Your Diabetes
and Live a Healthy Life

Recommended by The Canadian Diabetes Association

Understand Your Diabetes
and Live a Healthy Life

Diabetes Day-Care Unit – CHUM - Hôtel-Dieu, Montreal

New Edition 2009
(Translation of the 7th French Edition)

 ROGERS

© Rogers Media, 2009
1200 McGill College Avenue, suite 800
Montreal, Quebec H3B 4G7
Tel.: 514-843-2570 / Fax: 514-843-2183

Legal deposit : 2st quarter
Bibliothèque nationale du Québec, 2009
National Library of Canada, 2009
ISBN 978-2-922260-28-1

The publication of this work was made possible thanks to an unrestricted
educational grant from sanofi-aventis.

Editor:
Chantal Benhamron
Graphic Design and Layout:
Rogers Business and Professional Publishing Group

Preface

This publication is offered as a support for people who have recently been diagnosed with diabetes and for those who are taking the steps required to live an active and productive life as persons with diabetes. Diabetes is challenging, there is no doubt about it, and this is particularly true now, as new medications, technologies and informations are transforming our understanding of how Canadians can better care for themselves as they manage and treat their condition. Knowledge is the first and most important step.

This New edition 2009 of *Understand Your Diabetes and Live a Healthy Life* is an excellent resource. The information it contains is aimed at assisting people with diabetes in adopting healthy lifestyles and maintaining glucose levels that will delay and/or prevent both short- and long-term complications. Our mission at the Canadian Diabetes Association is to promote the health of Canadians through diabetes research, education, service and advocacy, and we recognize the importance of resources such as this publication as part of a support network for people with diabetes. On behalf of the Association, I applaud the authors' efforts in developing this new edition of *Understand Your Diabetes and Live a Healthy Life.*

Karen Philp
Vice-President
Public Policy and Government Relations
Canadian Diabetes Association

From the same publisher*

Dr. Michael McCormack and Dr. Fred Saad
Understanding Prostate Cancer (2008)

Dr. Michael McCormack and Dr. Fred Saad
Diagnosis and Management of Prostatic Diseases (2006)

Dr. André-H. Dandavino et al.
The Family Guide to Symptoms, 2nd edition (2003)

Dr. Michael McCormack
Male Sexual Health (2003)

Dr. André-H. Dandavino et al.
The Family Guide to Health Problems (2000)

Dr. Jacques Boulay
Bilingual Guide to Medical Abbreviations, 3rd edition (1998)

* All the above titles are also available in French.

Foreword

Here is another edition of *Understand Your Diabetes and Live a Healthy Life*, revised to include the Canadian Diabetes Association 2008 Clinical Practice Guidelines.

Diabetes has a long history. The Ancient Greeks used the term *dia-baino*, which means "to pass through", to describe people who urinated as soon as they took a drink. Thankfully, our understanding of diabetes, its causes, diagnosis, complications, treatment and prevention has never stopped evolving. It is now possible to prevent or delay the onset of type 2 diabetes through healthy living and certain medications.

It is very important for people with diabetes or at risk of developing the disease to be aware of new discoveries and approaches. This type of knowledge can help them change their lifestyles and make it easier to take control of this chronic disease, which is rapidly increasing in occurrence.

We hope that this book will be a valuable source of information for the population in general. More specifically, we hope that it can motivate people with diabetes to achieve a better understanding of themselves in relation to the disease and learn how to improve their treatment in order to get the most out of life.

CHUM–Hôtel-Dieu Diabetes Day-Care Unit Team

Acknowledgments

We would like to thank the members of the Division of Endocrinology-Metabolism and Nutrition of the CHUM-Hôtel-Dieu for their contribution, and to Ms. Susanne Bordeleau for her work as coordinator.

We would also like to express our gratitude to the following health professionals for their revisions, comments, and suggestions:

- Marc Aras, Director of Communications, Diabetes Québec
- Andrée Gagné, dietician, Diabetes Québec
- Julie Lalancette, dietician, Hôpital Charles-LeMoyne
- Carole Lavoie, Ph.D., professor, Department of Human Kinetics, Université du Québec à Trois-Rivières
- Catherine Noulard, dietician, CHUM
- Thérèse Surprenant, dietician, CHUM
- Julie St-Jean, dietician, Diabetes Québec
- Louise Tremblay, nurse and M.Ed., Diabetes Québec

List of Authors

This book has been re-edited by the multidisciplinary team of the Centre hospitalier de l'Université de Montréal, Hôtel-Dieu, namely:

- Françoise Desrochers, nurse clinician
- Lyne Gauthier, pharmacist
- Michelle Messier, dietician
- Hortensia Mircescu, endocrinologist
- Charles Tourigny, psychologist

We would also like to acknowledge the work done by the authors who contributed to previous editions:

- Nathalie Beaulieu, dietician
- Jean-Louis Chiasson, endocrinologist
- Julie Demers, pharmacist
- Micheline Fecteau-Côté, dietician
- Sylvie Fournier, pharmacist
- Christiane Gobeil, dietician
- Nicole Hamel, pharmacist
- Lise Lussier, psychologist
- Caroline Rivest, pharmacist
- Danièle Tremblay, psychologist
- Francis Viguié, psychologist

Objectives of This Book

This book has the following objectives:

General objective

To help people with diabetes achieve optimal control of their health so that they may improve their well-being and reduce the risk of developing complications of diabetes.

Specific objectives

To provide tools to people with diabetes to help them improve their habits, maintain normal blood glucose levels, and enable them to:

1) acquire general knowledge about diabetes;
2) adapt their diet to their diabetes and their various activities;
3) take into account the effects of stress and physical exercise on the management of their disease;
4) recognize the complications caused by poorly controlled blood glucose levels;
5) take effective steps when complications do occur;
6) recognize situations that require emergency intervention;
7) understand the treatments (such as drugs and insulin) that are used to treat diabetes and its complications;
8) understand the adjustments necessary in special situations (for example, while exercising or on trips);
9) understand the importance of good foot care and general hygiene;
10) correctly operate blood glucose measurement and insulin delivery devices;
11) use community resources, when needed;
12) adopt a positive attitude and management strategies to take better control of their health.

Table of Contents

General Information about Diabetes

1. What is diabetes?

Diabetes is a disease characterized by a lack of insulin and/or impaired insulin action, which causes an **elevation of blood glucose** (blood sugar) to levels above normal.

2. How many Canadians are affected by diabetes?

About **1.8 million Canadians** (5.5% of the population) had diabetes in 2005. It is anticipated that the number of cases will be 2.4 million by 2016, making diabetes the **disease of the 21st century.**

Engendering increasingly significant costs, diabetes is a growing societal problem, which must be battled on all fronts.

3. What are the criteria of a diagnosis of diabetes?

The diagnosis of diabetes is based on the following laboratory results from tests performed on venous blood:

1) **fasting blood glucose** equal to or above 7.0 mmol/L;
2) **random blood glucose** equal to or above 11.1 mmol/L;
3) **oral glucose tolerance test (OGTT)**, with a blood glucose level equal to or above 11.1 mmol/L two hours after the consumption of 75 g of glucose.

If there are no symptoms, however, a medical diagnosis of diabetes requires that an abnormal result on one of these tests be confirmed by repeating any one of the tests on a different day.

4. What is normal blood glucose?

Blood glucose is considered normal when it remains steady **between 4 mmol/L and 6 mmol/L before meals, and between 5 mmol/L and 8 mmol/L two hours after meals.**

5. What blood glucose levels are targeted in the treatment of diabetes?

The **target glucose levels** for most people with diabetes should be between 4 mmol/L and 7 mmol/L before meals, and between 5 mmol/L and 10 mmol/L two hours after meals. Target glucose levels after the meals should be tailored to the patient. If diabetes control is not optimal (glycated hemoglobin more than 7% or 0.070) target blood glucose level should be between 5 mmol/L and 8 mmol/L.

6. Why is it important to achieve a normal or target blood glucose level?

The closer blood glucose is to normal, the more a person with diabetes will:

1) feel **fit**, and
2) **lower the risk** of long-term complications associated with diabetes.

7. Why do blood glucose levels increase in a person with diabetes?

Blood glucose rises because of a **lack of insulin**, which can be caused by reduced insulin secretion, decreased insulin action, or a combination of the two. When there is **insufficient insulin** or insulin action to cause glucose to enter the cells, glucose levels in the blood increase. This is called **hyperglycemia**.

8. What is insulin?

Insulin is a hormone produced by the **pancreas**, an organ located in the abdomen, behind the stomach.

Insulin is like a **key that opens the door and lets glucose enter the cells**, which in turn lowers blood glucose levels.

9. How does the body use glucose?

Glucose is a vital **energy source** for the body's cells, much as gasoline is an important fuel for cars.

10. Where does excess glucose in the blood of a person with diabetes come from?

Excess glucose in the blood comes from two main sources:

1) foods containing **carbohydrates in meals and snacks;**
2) the **liver**, which produces glucose, when it makes too much.

11. What are the characteristics of type 1 diabetes?

Type 1 diabetes is typically characterized by the following features:

1) a **total lack of insulin;**
2) the appearance of the disease **around puberty** or in early adulthood (**usually before age 40**)
3) **weight loss;**
4) the need for treatment with **insulin injections.**

12. What are the characteristics of type 2 diabetes?

Type 2 diabetes is typically characterized by the following features:

1) **insulin resistance**, where the insulin produced becomes less effective;
2) **insufficient insulin production;**
3) appearance of the disease **after age 40** (although in certain populations at risk, it is becoming increasingly frequent in younger people);
4) **excess weight;**
5) significant **family history;**
6) treatment through lifestyle modification (dietary program, increased physical activity) **alone** or in combination with **oral antidiabetic drugs. In some cases, insulin injections are necessary.**

13. Are some people predisposed to diabetes?

Yes. Susceptibility to diabetes is inherited genetically.

14. Are there factors that can trigger diabetes in people who are predisposed to the disease?

Yes, there are a number of external (i.e. non genetic) factors that can trigger the disease in those with a predisposition.

Certain viral infections, for example, can precipitate type 1 diabetes in people who are predisposed. As for type 2 diabetes, two major factors play roles in its development: excess weight and lack of physical activity. Physical or physiological stress, such as heart attacks, strokes, or infections, can also trigger the development of diabetes, especially type 2, in predisposed individuals. It can also be brought on by psychological stressors, such as the loss of a loved one. Certain drugs, such high doses of cortisone or antipsychotics, can also be triggers.

15. Can some diseases cause diabetes?

Yes, certain diseases can cause diabetes. Cystic fibrosis and pancreatitis (inflammation of the pancreas) can destroy the pancreas, bringing on the disease. Other conditions, such as gestational diabetes, polycystic ovary syndrome, schizophrenia and certain types of muscular dystrophy also increase the risk of developing type 2 diabetes.

16. Are there tests to identify people who are predisposed to developing type 2 diabetes?

There are tests to identify people with an elevated risk of developing the disease.

A fasting blood glucose level above 6 mmol/L but below 7 mmol/L is considered an **abnormal fasting blood glucose level**; this phenomenon is called **impaired fasting blood glucose (IFG)**. An oral glucose tolerance test, which involves drinking a beverage containing 75 g of glucose on an empty stomach, can indicate **impaired glucose tolerance (IGT)** if blood glucose is measured anywhere between 7.8 mmol/L and 11.0 mmol/L two hours after the test.

These two conditions—**impaired fasting blood glucose and impaired glucose tolerance**—are considered pre-diabetic states and indicate an elevated risk of developing the disease.

Reactive hypoglycemia (below-normal blood glucose, usually three to four hours after a meal containing carbohydrates) is sometimes the first sign of type 2 diabetes.

17. Is it possible to prevent or slow down the development of diabetes in pre-diabetic people?

Yes. It has been shown that weight loss and physical activity can decrease the risk of developing type 2 diabetes by over 50% in people who are glucose intolerant. Certain medications (metformin, acarbose, thiazolidinediones) have also been shown to be effective, decreasing the risk of developing diabetes in subjects with impaired glucose tolerance by over 30%.

18. How can a person with diabetes achieve and maintain a target or normal blood glucose level?

To control their disease, people with diabetes have to take responsibility for it. The following guidelines can help:

1) **acknowledge and accept** the condition;
2) **eat** healthy food;
3) **lose weight**, if necessary;
4) be **physically active**;
5) measure **blood glucose** regularly;
6) take oral antidiabetic **drugs** and/or insulin as prescribed;
7) learn to **manage** stress;
8) stay well **informed** about diabetes.

o As the person with diabetes, you are the one person best equipped to manage it—along with the help and support of your doctor and other health care professionals.

o Diabetes is a chronic disease; it cannot be cured, but it can be controlled.

o You have done nothing to bring on your diabetes, and you have nothing to feel guilty about.

o The closer you keep your blood glucose to normal, the better you will feel.

o The more you learn about diabetes, the better able you will be to take responsibility for your condition.

Hyperglycemia

1. What is hyperglycemia?
Hyperglycemia occurs when **blood glucose rises above target levels** (above 7mmol/L before meals and 10 mmol two hours after meals).

2. How do people with diabetes develop hyperglycemia?
People with diabetes develop hyperglycemia when there is an **insufficient amount of insulin in the blood to handle the amount of glucose being released into the bloodstream.**

3. What are the symptoms of hyperglycemia?
When blood glucose rises above a certain threshold, the following symptoms can appear:
1) **increase in the volume of urine and the frequency of urination;**
2) intense **thirst;**
3) dry **mouth;**
4) excessive **hunger;**
5) involuntary **weight loss.**

Hyperglycemia can also cause the following symptoms:
6) **blurred vision;**
7) **infections**, especially of the genital organs and bladder;
8) **sores or wounds** that do not heal;
9) **fatigue;**
10) **drowsiness;**
11) **irritability.**

4. What are the main causes of hyperglycemia?

The main causes of hyperglycemia are:

1) over-consumption of **foods** containing carbohydrates;
2) **a decrease in physical activity**;
3) **incorrect dosage of** antidiabetic drugs (insulin or pills);
4) an **infection** or other medical conditions, such as a heart attack, that impair the secretion/action of insulin;
5) poor **stress** management;
6) taking certain **medications** (for example, cortisone);
7) uncorrected **nocturnal hypoglycemia** (low blood sugar) followed by a hyperglycemic rebound in the morning.

5. What should a person with diabetes do when hyperglycemia is suspected?

When hyperglycemia is suspected, blood glucose must be measured to confirm.

If hyperglycemia is confirmed, the following steps are necessary:

1) **people with type 1 diabetes must check for ketone bodies** if blood glucose is higher than 14 mmol/L. Reagent strips (Ketostix®) are used to measure the level of ketone bodies in the urine, and a meter (such as the Precision Xtra®) is used to measure the level of ketone bodies in a blood sample taken from the fingertip;
2) **drink plenty of water** to avoid dehydration (250 mL of water per hour, unless contraindicated);
3) identify the cause of the hyperglycemia;
4) correct the cause if possible;
5) continue eating (including carbohydrates) and follow the prescribed treatment (oral antidiabetic drugs or insulin);
6) call the doctor if the situation does not correct itself;
7) call the doctor or go to the emergency room if:
   o blood glucose rises above 20 mmol/L;
   o liquids taken orally cannot be retained because of nausea and vomiting;
   o the level of ketone bodies in the urine is moderate (4 mmol/L) to large (16 mmol/L); or
   o the level of ketone bodies in a blood sample taken from the fingertip is above 3 mmol/L.

6.   **What are the long-term complications of hyperglycemia?**

In the long term, hyperglycemia can cause complications affecting the eyes, kidneys, nerves, heart and blood vessels.

Hypoglycemia and Glucagon

1. **What is hypoglycemia?**
   Hypoglycemia is a **drop in blood glucose levels below normal** (below 4 mmol/L).

2. **Why does a person with diabetes develop hypoglycemia?**
   A person with diabetes develops hypoglycemia when there is **too much insulin in the blood in relation to the amount of glucose entering the circulation**.

3. **Who is susceptible to hypoglycemia?**
   People **who inject insulin or who take medications that stimulate the pancreas to produce more insulin can develop hypoglycemia**. Such medications include chlorpropamide (Apo®-Chlorpropamide), tolbutamide (Apo®-Tolbutamide), glyburide (Diaβeta®, Euglucon®), gliclazide (Diamicron® and Diamicron® MR), glimepiride (Amaryl®), repaglinide (GlucoNorm®) and nateglinide (Starlix®).

4. **What are the symptoms of hypoglycemia?**
   The body has two types of warning systems. The first causes symptoms with **rapid onset**, brought on by the secretion of adrenalin.

When hypoglycemia develops **rapidly**, it can cause the following symptoms:
1) **tremors or shakes;**
2) **palpitations;**
3) **sweating;**
4) **anxiety;**
5) **acute hunger;**
6) **pallor;**
7) **nightmares and restless sleep, if the hypoglycemia occurs during sleep;**
8) waking with a **headache** and **rebound hyperglycemia in the morning** following uncorrected nocturnal hypoglycemia during the previous night's sleep.

The second warning system creates less perceptible symptoms with **slower onset**. These symptoms are caused by a shortage of glucose being transported to the brain.

When hypoglycemia occurs **slowly**, the symptoms are more subtle:
1) **numbness or tingling around the mouth;**
2) **yawning;**
3) **fatigue or weakness;**
4) **the urge to sleep;**
5) **mood swings;**
6) **aggressiveness;**
7) **dizziness;**
8) **blurred vision;**
9) **unsteady gait, poor coordination;**
10) **difficulty pronouncing words;**
11) **confusion.**

5. Does hypoglycemia always cause these symptoms?

No. The symptoms of hypoglycemia vary from one person to another and can change over time. In some cases people with diabetes develop asymptomatic hypoglycemia, especially if blood glucose decreases slowly or the person has had diabetes for many years and no longer easily senses the hypoglycemia – a situation called hypoglycemia unawareness. The more frequent the hypoglycemia, the more likely it is that warning symptoms will appear later on and the correction of the problem will be delayed.

6.   What are the causes of hypoglycemia?

The most common causes of hypoglycemia can be broken down into four categories:

1) **food**
   - skipping a snack or a meal;
   - delaying a meal;
   - insufficient consumption of foods containing carbohydrates;
   - an error in measuring the carbohydrate content of food;
   - inability to keep food down or rapid loss (vomiting, diarrhea);
   - drinking alcohol (this can lead to hypoglycemia as long as 16 hours after consumption);
   - fasting while taking antidiabetic medications;
   - gastroparesis (delayed emptying of the contents of the stomach);
2) **physical activity**
   - physical activity without adjusting the intake of food or medication;
3) **antidiabetic drugs**
   - incorrect (excessive) dosage of antidiabetic drugs or insulin;
   - overcorrection of elevated blood glucose by the injection of an excessive dose of insulin;
   - failure to adjust to a lower dosage, despite glucose levels frequently lower than 4 mmol/L;
   - improper timing of antidiabetic drug doses.

7.   What should people with diabetes do if hypoglycemia is suspected?

If a person with diabetes suspects the onset of hypoglycemia, he or she **must not go to sleep** and assume that the blood glucose level will correct itself. Rather, the person must:

1) **measure blood glucose;**
2) **eat food with 15 g of rapidly absorbed carbohydrates.** Glucose or sucrose in pill or liquid form is the best option;
3) **wait 15 minutes;**
4) **measure blood glucose again;** if hypoglycemia is still present, **consume an additional 15 g of carbohydrates.**

If the hypoglycemia is corrected but the next meal is over an hour away, have a snack containing 15 g of carbohydrates and a protein source (e.g., 300 mL of milk or 7 soda crackers and cheese or fruit and cheese).

Note: Do not overtreat hypoglycemia as one risks getting hyperglycemia.

If the person with diabetes is **unable to administer his or her own treatment**:
1) measure his or her blood glucose level, if possible;
2) give the person food containing **20 g of carbohydrates** (if person able to swallow);
3) repeat after 15 minutes, giving the person food with 15 g of carbohydrates if blood glucose remains lower than 4 mmol/L.

Examples of foods with **15 g of carbohydrates**:
1ˢᵗ choice (rapidly absorbed)
- o 3 tablets of Glucose BD® (1 tablet = 5 g of carbohydrates)
- o 4 tables of Dex4® (1 tablet = 4 g of carbohydrates); gel or liquid available
- o 5 tablets of Dextrosol® (1 tablet = 3 g of carbohydrates)
- o 7 tablets of Glucosol® (1 tablet = 2.25 g of carbohydrates)
- o 125 mL (½ cup) of regular (not diet) soft drink (pop) or fruit beverage
- o 5 mL (3 tsp or 3 packets) of sugar dissolved in water
- o 15 mL (3 tsp) of honey, jam or syrup
- o Insta-Glucose® (1 tube = 24 g of carbohydrates; take the equivalent of 15 g)

2ⁿᵈ choice (slower absorption)
- o 125 mL (½ cup) of fruit juice without added sugar
- o 300 mL (1¼ cups) of milk
- o 200 mL (1 single-serving size carton) of milk with 2 Social Tea biscuits
- o 4 Social Tea biscuits
- o 7 soda crackers
- o 1 dried fruit bar (for example, "Fruit To Go")
- o 1 small apple or 1/2 banana or 2 kiwis or 2 dates, etc.

Examples of quickly absorbed foods containing **20 g of carbohydrates**:
- o 4 tablets of Glucose BD® (1 tablet = 5 g of carbohydrates)
- o 5 tablets of Dex4® (1 tablet = 4 g of carbohydrates)
- o 7 tablets of Dextrosol® (1 tablet = 3 g of carbohydrates)
- o 9 tablets of Glucosol® (1 tablet = 2.25 g of carbohydrates)
- o 175 mL (3/4 cup) of regular soft drink (not diet) or fruit beverage
- o 20 mL (4 tsp) or 4 packets of sugar dissolved in water
- o 20 mL (4 tsp) of honey, jam or syrup
- o Insta-Glucose (1 tube = 24 g of carbohydrates; take the equivalent of 20 g)

8. **Why is it important to treat hypoglycemia immediately?**

Hypoglycemia must be treated **immediately**; if left uncorrected, hypoglycemia can lead to loss of consciousness, coma and sometimes convulsions. There is no such thing as "minor hypoglycemia".

9. **Does uncorrected hypoglycemia always lead to coma?**

No, uncorrected hypoglycemia does not necessarily lead to coma. The body attempts to defend itself from hypoglycemia by secreting hormones such as glucagon and adrenalin, which can elevate blood glucose and correct hypoglycemia. If there is too much insulin in the blood, however, these efforts might not be sufficient to correct hypoglycemia and prevent coma.

10. **How can hypoglycemia be avoided?**

The following precautions are usually effective in avoiding hypoglycemia:
1) measure blood glucose regularly;
2) keep regular mealtime hours and include foods containing carbohydrates;
3) check blood glucose before undertaking any physical activity and consume carbohydrates as necessary (*see chapter 20 on physical activity*);
4) avoid consuming alcohol on an empty stomach;
5) check blood glucose around 2 a.m., if necessary because one suspects nocturnal hypoglycemia;
6) take antidiabetic drugs as prescribed, following the recommended dosage and timetable.

Note: People with type 1 diabetes are advised to periodically check blood glucose around 2 a.m. A snack containing at least 15 g of carbohydrates and a protein source is also recommended before turning in for the night if blood glucose is below 7 mmol/L at bedtime.

11. **What safety measures should be taken by people with diabetes who are at risk for hypoglycemia?**

People with diabetes at risk for hypoglycemia must:
1) always have at least **two 15 g servings of carbohydrates within reach**;
2) wear a diabetic ID **bracelet** or **pendant**;

3) **inform** family, friends and colleagues that they have diabetes and tell them about the symptoms of hypoglycemia and the way to deal with it;
4) if they take insulin, always have **glucagon** within reach at home, at work or when travelling. A friend or relative must learn how to inject the glucagon in the event of a hypoglycemic coma.

12. What should be done if a person with diabetes has fallen into a hypoglycemic coma?

If a person with diabetes is unconscious or in a hypoglycemic coma, another person must immediately:
- inject him or her with glucagon, if available; if not,
- call for an ambulance by dialling 911.

Never try to feed sugary foods to an unconscious person. Food can be inhaled into the lungs instead of being swallowed into the stomach.

13. What is glucagon?

Glucagon is a hormone produced by the pancreas to elevate blood glucose. In the event of a hypoglycemic coma, glucagon must be injected by another person to correct the hypoglycemia.

A glucagon injection first-aid kit should always be on hand; it can be stored at room temperature. Check the expiry date periodically.

Here are the steps to follow in the event of a hypoglycemic coma:
1) lay the person on his or her side (glucagon can occasionally cause nausea and vomiting);
2) remove the plastic cap from the bottle of glucagon;
3) remove the needle sheath and inject the entire contents of the syringe into the bottle of glucagon. Do not remove the plastic stop ring from the syringe. Remove the syringe from the bottle;
4) gently shake the bottle until the glucagon powder is completely dissolved in the solvent;
5) draw up all of the solution from the vial using the same syringe;

6) inject the contents of the syringe (1 mg) subcutaneously (under the skin) or intramuscularly. The person should awaken within 15 minutes. There is no risk of overdose. A doctor may recommend a half dose for children who weigh less than 20 kg (44 pounds);

7) give the person some food as soon as he or she is awake and able to swallow. Provide a substantial snack containing 45 g of carbohydrates and a protein source (e.g., orange juice and a meat sandwich or crackers and cheese);

8) inform the person's doctor of the incident so that treatment can be evaluated and possibly adjusted. A visit to the emergency room may still be necessary to follow-up on the correction of the hypoglycemia.

> If the person with diabetes does not regain consciousness within 15 to 20 minutes after the glucagon injection, ensure that he or she is brought to the emergency room immediately.

14. What are the recommendations for people with diabetes who are at risk for nocturnal hypoglycemia but live alone?

People with diabetes who live alone may be apprehensive of experiencing nocturnal hypoglycemia. It should be remembered, however, that hypoglycemia rarely persists for extended periods of time. In a crisis situation, the body reacts by raising the blood glucose level using sugar stored in the liver. Nevertheless, the situation is stressful. In addition to taking preventive measures to avoid a crisis, a person with diabetes should also have a social network in place to ensure his or her safety in case of prolonged hypoglycemia. Here are some suggestions:

1) ask a friend or relative to telephone every morning;

2) ask the mailman to deliver the mail in person;

3) agree on a code system with a neighbour (for example, one curtain open or closed upon waking);

4) use a personal response telephone service with a two-way voice communication system such as Philips Lifeline: 514-735-2101 or 1 877 423-9700.

> It is a good idea to leave a house key with a friend or relative who can help if necessary.

15. Can symptoms of hypoglycemia occur when blood glucose is normal?

Yes, there are two situations in which a person with diabetes can have symptoms of hypoglycemia when blood glucose is normal:

1) When hyperglycemia has existed for some time, using antidiabetic medications to normalize blood glucose levels too quickly can trigger symptoms of hypoglycemia sometimes lasting several days. To avoid this unpleasant feeling, it may be necessary to slow down the treatment so that blood sugar can decrease more gradually. The ultimate goal is always to regain a normal blood glucose level.

2) When blood glucose is quite elevated and then quickly drops to a normal level, symptoms of hypoglycemia may appear and then fade quickly. Therefore, if hypoglycemia is suspected, blood glucose levels must be tested to avoid treating a false case of hypoglycemia, which could cause the hyperglycemia to recur.

16. Is reactive hypoglycemia a sign of diabetes?

Reactive hypoglycemia is sometimes the first sign of type 2 diabetes. This type of hypoglycemia usually appears three or four hours after a meal containing carbohydrates — hence the term "reactive". In general, reactive hypoglycemia corrects itself spontaneously, even if no carbohydrates are ingested.

o The symptoms or signs of hypoglycemia do not always occur simultaneously.

o The symptoms of hypoglycemia can differ from one person to another ou from person to person.

o Symptoms and discomforts can change over time. When a person has had diabetes for 10 to 20 years, he or she may no longer experience the symptoms of hypoglycemia (neuropathy).

o The symptoms of hypoglycemia can be masked by certain medications, such as beta-blockers.

o The symptoms of hypoglycemia may be absent if the person suffers from repeated episodes leading to hypoglycemia unawareness.

o Certain signs and symptoms of hypoglycemia are difficult to assess. Glucose levels should therefore be confirmed with a glucose meter to avoid making unnecessary correction.

o Hypoglycemia should be corrected immediately, following the recommended steps, to ensure that there is no damage to the brain. It should be remembered that hypoglycemia, no matter how severe or mild, must always be taken seriously.

RECOMMENDATIONS FOR THE TREATMENT OF HYPOGLYCEMIA FOR PEOPLE WITH DIABETES

↓

Test blood glucose immediately

↓

If blood glucose is lower than 4.0 mmol/L

1. If no assistance is required for treatment, take 15 g of carbohydrates in one of the appropriate forms:

1st choice (absorbed quickly)

   o   3 tablets of Glucose BD® (1 tablet = 5 g of carbohydrates)
   o   4 tablets of Dex4® (1 tablet = 4 g of carbohydrates); gel or liquid available
   o   5 tablets of Dextrosol® (1 tablet = 3 g of carbohydrates)
   o   7 tablets of Glucosol® (1 tablet = 2.25 g of carbohydrates)
   o   125 mL (½ cup) of regular soft drink or fruit beverage
   o   15 mL (3 tsp. or 3 packets) of sugar dissolved in water
   o   15 mL (3 tsp.) of honey, jam or syrup
   o   Insta-Glucose® (1 tube = 24 g of carbohydrates, take the equivalent of 15 g)

2nd choice (absorbed more slowly)

   o   125 mL (½ cup) fruit juice without added sugar
   o   300 mL (1 ¼ cup) of milk
   o   200 mL (1 single-serving carton) of milk plus 2 dry Social Tea biscuits
   o   4 dry Social Tea biscuits
   o   7 soda crackers
   o   1 dry fruit bar (for example, "Fruit to go")
   o   1 small apple, ½ banana, 2 kiwis, or 2 dates, etc.

2. If the person is conscious but needs assistance for treatment, give him or her 20 g of carbohydrates in the appropriate form:

   o   4 tablets of Glucose BD® (1 tablet = 5 g of carbohydrates)
   o   5 tablets of Dex4® (1 tablet = 4 g of carbohydrates)
   o   7 tablets of Dextrosol® (1 tablet = 3 g of carbohydrates)
   o   9 tablets of Glucosol® (1 tablet = 2.25 g of carbohydrates)

o   175 mL (¾ cup) of regular soft drink or fruit beverage

o   20 mL (4 tsp. or 4 packets) of sugar dissolved in water

o   20 mL (4 tsp.) of honey, jam or syrup

o   Insta-Glucose® (1 tube = 24 g of carbohydrates; take the equivalent of 20 g)

↓

Wait 15 minutes and test blood glucose again

↓

**If blood glucose is still below 4.0 mmol/L,
have another 15 g of carbohydrates**

↓

Wait 15 minutes, and repeat treatment as needed

↓

When blood glucose reaches or exceeds 4.0 mmol/L

↓

Meal (or snack) expected within one hour or less

↓   ↓

Yes   **No**

Have the meal or snack as planned   **Have a snack containing 15 g of
carbohydrates and a protein source
(e.g., 200 mL of milk plus 2 Social Tea
biscuits) while waiting for the meal**

3. If the person is unconscious:

o   Inject 1 mg of Glucagon SC or IM
     (dosage for adults and children weighing more than 20 kg (44 pounds).

o   When the person has regained consciousness and is able to swallow,
     provide a substantial snack of 45 g of carbohydrates and a protein source
     (e.g., orange juice and a meat sandwich or cheese and crackers).

CAUTION

1. For people with diabetes taking acarbose (Glucobay®) in combination with other medications that may cause hypoglycemia, the hypoglycemia should be corrected in one of the following ways:
   - 3 tablets of Glucose BD® (1 tablet = 5 g of carbohydrates)
   - 4 tablets of Dex4® (1 tablet = 4 g of carbohydrates); gel or liquid available
   - 5 tablets of Dextrosol® (1 tablet = 3 g of carbohydrates)
   - 300 mL (1 1/4 cups) of milk
   - 15 mL (3 tsp) of honey

2. For people with diabetes suffering from **kidney problems**, hypoglycemia should be corrected in one of the following ways:
   - 3 tablets of Glucose BD® (1 tablet = 5 g of carbohydrates)
   - 4 tablets of Dex4® (1 tablet = 4 g of carbohydrates); gel or liquid available
   - 5 tablets of Dextrosol® (1 tablet = 3 g of carbohydrates)
   - 3 packets of sugar dissolved in a little water

3. Hypoglycemia should never be dismissed as minor or unimportant. All appropriate measures should be taken to prevent it. When it occurs, it should be treated immediately.

Self-monitoring:

Blood Glucose and Glycosylated Hemoglobin (A1C)

1. What is self-monitoring?

Self-monitoring is a technique that people with diabetes use to **measure their own blood glucose levels**. Consequently, the approach usually also includes **adjusting** treatment according to the results obtained to bring and maintain blood glucose levels as close to normal as possible.

2. Why practice self-monitoring?

Self-monitoring allows people with diabetes to:

1) measure the impact of **nutrition, physical activity, stress and antidiabetic drugs** on blood glucose;
2) identify episodes of hypoglycemia and hyperglycemia and react quickly;
3) modify their behaviour with respect to nutrition, physical activity, antidiabetic drugs and stress, as required;
4) measure the impact of these changes on blood glucose;
5) feel confident, safe and independent in the management of their diabetes; and above all,
6) bring and maintain blood glucose levels as close to normal as possible.

3. Why should people with diabetes try to maintain blood glucose levels as close to normal as possible?

People with diabetes should try to maintain their blood glucose levels as close as possible to normal to prevent complications associated with diabetes.

Two major studies (one American study on type 1 diabetes and one British study on type 2 diabetes) have shown that maintaining blood glucose levels as close to normal as possible significantly reduces the development and progression of microvascular complications due to diabetes:

- o Retinopathy: decrease of 21% to 76%
- o Nephropathy: decrease of 34% to 54%
- o Neuropathy: decrease of 40% to 60% or improvement in the existing neuropathy

4. How is blood glucose measured from the fingertip?

A glucose meter is used to measure blood glucose in blood from the fingertip. The procedure involves two steps:

Preparing the materials and checking the reagent strips

1) **Wash your hands** with soapy water and dry them thoroughly. This reduces the risk of infection and makes it easier to take the blood sample. Alcohol swabs are not recommended for home use because they can dry out the skin, which can lead to cracked fingertips.
2) **Prepare the materials**: meter, test strip, holder, lancet, paper tissue.
3) **Insert the lancet into the holder** and set it. A lancet must never be used more than once. It should not be thrown directly into the ordinary trashcan. Special containers are distributed at no charge in pharmacies and Community Health Centres. Once a container is full, it can be returned for safe disposal. **Never use a lancet or a holder that another person has already used.**
4) Check the reagent strip container for the manufacturer's expiration date.
5) If appropriate, write the date of first opening on the container to **keep track of the life expectancy of the strips.**
6) **Take out a test strip.** If the strip comes from a vial, close it immediately.

Blood analysis and recording of data

1) Press the switch to start the device, if necessary.
2) Insert the test strip into the strip support on the device or automatically release a strip from the device.
3) Prick the **lateral extremity** of a finger (use a different finger each time you take a blood sample).
4) Produce a **large drop of blood** by applying pressure on the finger while pointing it downwards. Do not apply excessive pressure.
5) Place the **first drop of blood** on the reactive part of the strip or bring the reactive part of the strip into contact with the blood, depending on the device used.
6) Wait for the reading to be displayed.
7) Enter the result in the appropriate column of your glucose logbook.

5. Can other sites ("alternative sites") be used to measure blood glucose?

Blood glucose can be measured with blood drawn from other areas of the body ("alternate sites") such as the forearm, the arm, the palm, the abdomen or the thigh. Several glucose meters now offer this option.

Results from alternative sites are generally comparable to glucose readings taken from the fingertip before a meal. This method of measuring blood glucose is limited, however, and it is recommended that a blood glucose reading be taken from the fingertip at times when blood glucose can fluctuate rapidly. This can occur:

1) during an episode of hypoglycemia;
2) during physical activity;
3) up to two hours after a meal;
4) immediately after an insulin injection;
5) during an illness.

6. Which glucose meters are currently available, and what are their features?

The tables on pages 48 to 51 present a list of the latest generation of blood glucose meters on the market, along with some of their characteristics (list updated on January 1ˢᵗ 2009).

Blood glucose meters are frequently offered for free and many manufacturers will trade new meters for old ones at no cost. Continuous glucose monitors can cost as much as $2000.

Strips cost between $0.80 and $1.00 each. There are special offers on some strips. The price can also vary from one pharmacy to another.

7. What are the main causes of false glucose readings?

False readings occur when:
1) the glucose meter is dirty;
2) the glucose meter is calibrated incorrectly;
3) the user forgets to calibrate the meter, leaving out the calibration code for the current batch of reagent strips;
4) the strips have expired;
5) the strips have been exposed to humidity;
6) the strips have been exposed to extreme temperatures;
7) the strips are kept out of the original vial;
8) the drop of blood is too small;
9) the user's technique is faulty (e.g., the time of contact with the strip is too short);
10) the glucose meter is inaccurate.

8. How can the accuracy of glucose meter results be verified?

The accuracy of results taken from the glucose meter should be verified annually. The **fasting blood glucose** level from a laboratory blood test should be compared with the level the patient obtains from the blood glucose meter. Blood glucose should be tested **within five minutes after** the blood sample.

The result of the **fasting blood glucose** reading from a blood glucose meter should **vary by less than 20%** from the blood glucose reading taken in the laboratory. For glucose readings less than or equal to 4.2 mmol/L, the difference should be smaller.

HOW CAN THE ACCURACY OF A GLUCOSE METER BE MEASURED?

Fasting

1) Have a "fasting blood glucose" measured in the laboratory.
2) Take a glucose reading as usual, within the following five minutes.
3) Enter this information in the logbook and circle it.
4) Ask for the results of the blood test at the next visit to the doctor.
5) Calculate the accuracy of the meter (a difference of more or less 20%).

	Example	**Your results**
Fasting blood glucose (laboratory blood sample)	10 mmol/L	....
Blood glucose from fingertip (taken within 5 minutes)	9.2 mmol/L	....
Accuracy of the meter expressed as a percentage		................%

Formula for calculating the accuracy of meter

$$(9.2 - 10.0) \div 10.0$$

(9.2	**− 10.0)**	**÷ 10.0**
Blood glucose on fingertip with meter	Fasting blood glucose from blood test	Fasting blood glucose from blood test
Your result:	Your result:	Your result: ....

x 100 = 8%

Your result:
....

A difference of 20% or less is considered acceptable.
Aim for a smaller difference for blood glucose levels below 4.2 mmol/L.

9. How often should blood glucose levels be measured?

Generally, people with **type 1** diabetes or those who are currently in a period of adjustment are advised to measure blood glucose **at least three times a day** at various intervals: **before each meal and before bedtime** (before snacking). Sometimes, the doctor responsible for treatment will advise a patient to measure blood glucose two hours after meals (generally timing it from the first mouthful) and even during the night.

People with **non-insulin dependent type 2** diabetes are generally advised to measure blood glucose **once a day,** alternating between measurements before meals and measurements before bedtime (before a snack). On some occasions they are instructed to measure blood glucose two hours after meals (generally timing it from the first mouthful), and in some cases, even during the night. People who are in a period of adjustment or insulin-requiring are advised to measure blood glucose several times a day.

It is also a good idea to measure blood glucose whenever unease or discomfort suggests the **possibility of hypoglycemia** or **hyperglycemia**. In the case of illness, blood glucose should be measured more often.

Blood glucose levels should be tested more often whenever **any change occurs**, whether the change is in diet, medication or stress levels.

When engaging in **physical activity,** blood glucose should be measured before, during and afterwards.

People with diabetes are advised to take a blood glucose reading before **driving a car** and every four hours during long drives in order to prevent hypoglycemia.

10. What information should be recorded in the logbook to help self-monitor blood glucose?

Blood glucose self-monitoring is easier when the following information is recorded in the logbook:

1) the result and date of **blood glucose** readings (in the column corresponding to the meal in question; for example, "Before lunch");

2) relevant comments, such as the explanation for the **hypoglycemia**, change in diet, physical activity, etc.;

3) the result of a **ketone bodies** reading from urine or blood, with the date and time (in the "Comments" column);

4) the name, dose and time of ingestion of **all prescribed antidiabetic drugs**; write down every change or omission in the "Comments" column;

5) the quantity of carbohydrates consumed in meals and snacks;

6) the area of the insulin injection, if applicable, the technique used, and so on (in the "Comments" column).

11. How should the information be recorded?

The information should be noted in the **self-monitoring logbook**. Each reading category should be entered in a clearly identified column:

1) in the first column, write down the results of blood glucose readings taken **before the morning meal** over the course of a single week;

2) in the second column, write down the results of blood glucose readings taken **after the morning meal** over the course of a single week;

3) in the next columns, enter the results of the **other blood glucose readings**, taken before and after the afternoon and evening meals, before bedtime (before a snack) and during the night;

4) **hypoglycemia** occurring outside the four usual periods of blood glucose readings should be noted in the following period (e.g., hypoglycemia occurring in the afternoon should be entered in the column corresponding to "Before the evening meal");

5) unmeasured hypoglycemia should be assigned a reading of **2 mmol/L**;

6) the **weekly average** of glucose readings should be entered at the foot of each column (do not include the results of hypoglycemic correction when calculating the average). See the example indicated by two asterisks (**) in the table on the next page;

7) when calculating averages, do not include readings associated with an exceptional, one-off, explainable situation; see the examples indicated by an asterisk (*) in the table on the next page;

8) enter any relevant remarks in the "Comments" column.

Example of a self-monitoring logbook

Week beginning Sunday:		01 (day)		01 (month)		2009 (year)		
Day of the week	**Blood glucose measurements (mmol/L)**							**Comments**
	Breakfast		**Lunch**		**Dinner**		**Bedtime**	
	Before	After	Before	After	Before	After	Before snack	
Sunday	5.2		12.1					
Monday	7.1				8.1			
Tuesday	4.6						4.1	
Wednesday	9.3		10.4					
Thursday	5.5				7.2		6.7	
Friday	6.8				3.5*		16.6**	*Exercise **Corrected hypoglycemia
Saturday	3.9		11.3		18.1*			*Stress
Average	**6.1**		**11.3**		**7.7**		**5.4**	

The average is calculated by adding up all the numbers in the same column and dividing the total by the number of measurements in that column:

Example: Average blood glucose before lunch:
12.1 + 10.4 + 11.3 = 33.8 ÷ 3 = 11.3

12. Will the doctor prescribe other tests in addition to blood glucose readings to monitor blood glucose?

In addition to blood glucose readings, the doctor may prescribe blood tests to measure **glycosylated hemoglobin** or A1C and in some cases **fructosamine**. These two laboratory analyses show how well the diabetes has been managed.

1) Glycosylated hemoglobin or A1C

The glycosylated hemoglobin or AIC levels reflects how well blood glucose has been controlled over the last two to three months.

This type of hemoglobin results from the binding of blood glucose to the hemoglobin present in red blood cells. The higher the blood glucose, the higher the level of A1C, due to the binding of sugar molecules to hemoglobin.

A blood test is used to measure the A1C value. It should be done two to four times a year, depending on how well the diabetes is managed. The A1C value is essential information, giving people an overall picture of their blood glucose management and making it possible to adjust treatment. A1C is complementary to the blood glucose meter readings. A1C does not indicate requiring blood glucose variations, hypoglycemia or hyperglycemia. It is recommended to target an A1C value of 7% (0.070) or less. For some patients with type 2 diabetes, to further decrease the risk of renal damage, a target A1C equal or less than 6.5% (0.065) may be considered. This must be balanced against the risk of hypoglycaemia and the cardiovascular risk.

2) Fructosamine

Fructosamine levels reflect how well blood glucose has been controlled over the last two to three weeks.

Using fructosamine levels as a marker of the risk of complications of diabetes is a less well established practice. This kind of reading (which is carried out through a blood test) can nevertheless be useful in some cases, for example:

- o short-term assessments of a change in treatment;
- o assessment of blood glucose management when A1C levels are less reliable (e.g., in the presence of hemoglobin disease, severe anemia);
- o follow-up on blood glucose levels during pregnancy.

Normal fructosamine levels are generally considered to be between 200 and 290 µmol/L. Like A1C, fructosamine does not indicate blood glucose variations and is complementary to regular blood glucose measurements.

LIST OF BLOOD GLUCOSE METERS (REVISED JANUARY 1ST, 2009)

Blood glucose meter	Manufacturer	Range of results (mmol/L)	Range of temperature of strips (°C)	Length of test (sec.)
FreeStyle® Lite®	Abbott	1.1 to 27.8	4 to 40	5
FreeStyle® Freedom Lite®	Abbott	1.1 to 27.8	4 to 40	5
Precision Xtra® Blood glucose (G) Ketone bodies (K)	Abbott	G: 1.1 to 27.8 C: 0 to 6.0	15 to 40	G: 5 C: 10
iTest®	AgaMatrix Auto Control Medical	1.1 to 33.3	10 to 40	4
Ascensia® * Breeze 2®	Bayer	0.6 to 33.3	10 to 40	5
Ascensia® Contour® *	Bayer	0.6 to 33.3	10 to 40	5
OneTouch® UltraMini® (4 colours)	LifeScan	1.1 to 33.3	6 to 44	5
OneTouch® Ultra 2®	LifeScan	1.1 to 33.3	6 to 44	5
OneTouch® UltraSmart®	LifeScan	1.1 to 33.3	6 to 44	5
Guardian® ** REAL-Time	Medtronic MiniMed	2.2 to 22.2	sensors 2 to 27	Initialization: 2 hrs 20 mins; calibration: 2-3/day with meter; results every 5 mins
Nova Max®	Nova Biomedical	1.1 to 33.3	15 to 39	5
Accu-Chek® Aviva	Roche Diagnostics	0.6 to 33.3	4 to 44	5
Accu-Chek® Compact Plus®***	Roche Diagnostics	0.6 to 33.3	10 to 40	5

*   Speech synthesis is available at Pharmacie Danielle Desroches (905 Blvd. René-Lévesque E., tel: 514 288-8555 or 450 447-9280) for $495.
**   Continuous monitor costing $2,000, plus $47.50 for a 72-hour sensor.
***   Accu-Chek MC Voicemate Plus MC speech synthesis available for $300.

Blood glucose meter	Amount of blood required (μL)	Possibility of adding a second drop of blood	Cleaning required	Calibration of reactive strips	Lifespan of reactive strips
FreeStyle® Lite®	0.3	yes (within 60 seconds)	no	automatic	date on vial
FreeStyle® Freedom Lite®	0.3	yes (within 60 seconds)	no	automatic	date on vial
Precision Xtra® Blood glucose (G) Ketone bodies (K)	G: 0.6 C: 1.5	yes (within 5 seconds)	no	calibration strip in every box	date on the packet
iTest®	0.5	no	no	calibration code on every vial	3 months (after opening)
Ascensia®* Breeze 2®	1.0	no	no	automatic	date on disc
Ascensia® Contour®*	0.6	no	no	automatic	6 months (after opening)
OneTouch® UltraMini® (4 colours)	1.0	no	no	calibration code on every vial	3 months (after opening)
OneTouch® Ultra 2®	1.0	no	no	calibration code on every vial	3 months (after opening)
OneTouch® UltraSmart®	1.0	no	no	calibration code on every vial	3 months (after opening)
Guardian® ** REAL-Time	N/A	N/A	N/A	N/A	sensor lifespan: 72 hours ($47.50/sensor)
Nova Max®	0.3	no	no	no coding necessary	3 months (after opening)
Accu-Chek® Aviva	0.6	yes (within 5 seconds)	no	calibration chip in every box	date on vial
Accu-Chek® Compact Plus®****	1. 5	yes (within 25 seconds)	yes	automatic	3 months (after cartridge use)

Blood glucose meter	Reactive strips	Lifespan of control solution after opening	PC Programs/ Memory	Batteries and lifespan	Guarantee
FreeStyle® Lite®	in vial (sensitive to humidity)	3 months	400	1 lithium 3 V No. CR2032 500 tests	5 years
FreeStyle® Freedom Lite®	in vial (sensitive to humidity)	3 months	400	1 lithium 3 V no CR2032 1000 tests	5 years
Precision Xtra® Blood glucose (G) Ketone bodies (K)	individually wrapped	3 months	450	1 lithium 3 V No. CR2032 1000 tests	4 years
iTest®	in vial (sensitive to humidity)	3 months	300	2 lithium 3 V No. CR2032 1000 tests	4 years
Ascensia® * Breeze 2®	10-test disc	6 months	420	1 lithium 3 V No. CR2032 1000 tests	5 years
Ascensia® Contour® *	in vial (sensitive to humidity)	6 months	480	2 lithium 3 V No. CR2032 1000 tests	5 years
OneTouch® UltraMini® (4 colours)	in vial (sensitive to humidity)	3 months	500	1 lithium 3 V No. CR2032 1000 tests	3 years
OneTouch® Ultra 2®	in vial (sensitive to humidity)	3 months	500	2 lithium 3 V No. CR2032 1000 tests	3 years
OneTouch® UltraSmart®	in vial (sensitive to humidity)	3 months	3000	2 alkaline AAA, 1.5 V 540 tests	3 years
Guardian® ** REAL-Time	N/A	N/A	288 readings/day; 21 days of information	1 alkaline AAA, 1.5 V; 40 recharges of MiniLink 14 days	1 year
Nova Max®	in vial (sensitive to humidity)	3 months	400	1 lithium, 3 V No. CR2450, 500 test	3 years
Accu-Chek® Aviva	in vial (sensitive to humidity)	3 months	500	1 lithium, 3 V No. CR2032 less than 2000 tests	5 years
Accu-Chek® Compact Plus®****	17-strip cartridge	3 months	500	2 alkaline AAA, 1.5 V 1000 tests	5 years

Blood glucose meter	Alternative sites	Lancing device	Lancet	Telephone assistance	Internet
FreeStyle® Lite®	yes	FreeStyle	FreeStyle 25 gauge	1-888-519-6890	www.abbott.com
FreeStyle® Freedom Lite®	yes	FreeStyle	FreeStyle 25 gauge	1-888-519-6890	www.abbott.com
Precision Xtra® Blood glucose (G) Ketone bodies (K)	yes	Easy Touch	Abbott Thin Lancets 28 gauge	1-888-519-6890	www.abbott.com
iTest®	yes	iTest	iTest ultra-thin 33 gauge	1-800-461-0991	www.itestglucose. com
Ascensia®* Breeze 2®	yes	Microlet	Microlet 28 gauge	1-800-268-7200	www.ascensia.ca
Ascensia® Contour®*	yes	Microlet	Microlet 28 gauge	1-800-268-7200	www.ascensia.ca
OneTouch® UltraMini® (4 colours)	yes	OneTouch	OneTouch UltraSoft 28 gauge	1-800-663-5521	www.one touch.ca
OneTouch® Ultra 2®	yes	OneTouch	OneTouch UltraSoft 28 gauge	1-800-663-5521	www.one touch.ca
OneTouch® UltraSmart®	yes	OneTouch UltraSoft	OneTouch UltraSoft 28 gauge	1-800-663-5521	www.one touch.ca
Guardian® ** REAL-Time	N/A	N/A	N/A	1-866-444-4649	www.guardianreal time.ca
Nova Max®	yes	Nova	Nova automatic with alternate site testing cap 10 lancets	1-800-260-1021	www.nova cares.ca
Accu-Chek® Aviva	yes	Accu-Chek Multiclix	Accu-Chek Multiclix 30 gauge (6-lancet cartridge)	1-800-363-7949	www.accu-chek.ca
Accu-Chek® Compact Plus®***	yes	Softclix Plus	Accu-Chek Softclix 28 gauge	1-800-363-7949	www.accu-chek.ca

Measuring Ketone Bodies

1.   What are ketone bodies?
Ketone bodies are **by-products of the breakdown of body fat.**

2.   What does an increase of ketone bodies in the blood mean?
An increase of ketone bodies in the blood indicates that a **lack of insulin** is causing a person with diabetes to use **fat** reserves stored in the body instead of **glucose.**

Without insulin, many cells in the body are unable to use glucose in the blood. When the body lacks insulin, it uses energy stored in the form of fat, and the breakdown of this fat leads to the production of **ketone bodies**. Ketone bodies are acids; their presence can lead to **diabetic ketoacidosis.**

Excess ketone bodies in the blood are eliminated through the urine. They may therefore be measured in either blood or urine.

3.   Why must people with diabetes check for excess ketone bodies in the blood or urine?
People with diabetes—especially type 1—must check for excess ketone bodies in the blood or urine **because an excess indicates poor management of the disease** and a risk of diabetic ketoacidosis. Ketoacidosis can lead to coma. In some special cases, doctors recommend this type of monitoring for people with type 2 diabetes.

4. **When should people with diabetes check for excess ketone bodies in the blood or urine?**

People with diabetes should check for the presence of ketone bodies in the blood or urine when their **blood glucose is higher than 14 mmol/L or when a doctor recommends** it.

They should continue performing the test—in addition to measuring blood glucose four times a day or more often if necessary—until there are no excess **ketone bodies** in the **blood or urine and blood glucose is back to normal.**

They should also test for ketone bodies if they experience the following symptoms:
1) intense thirst;
2) abdominal pain;
3) excessive tiredness or drowsiness;
4) nausea and vomiting.

5. **What should a person with diabetes do if there are excess ketone bodies in the blood or urine?**

A person with diabetes who finds excess ketone bodies in the blood or urine should:
1) **drink 250 mL** of water every hour to hydrate and help eliminate ketone bodies through the urine;
2) **take extra doses of Apidra®, Humalog®, NovoRapid®, Humulin® R or Novolin® ge Toronto insulin, following the recommendations of the treating physician** (*see chapter 21 on hyperglycemic emergencies*);
3) call a doctor **immediately** or go to the emergency room if an excess of ketone bodies in the blood or urine persists despite treatment and if the following symptoms appear:
   o abdominal pain;
   o excessive tiredness or drowsiness;
   o nausea and vomiting.

6. **How is the presence of ketone bodies measured in urine?**

Ketone bodies in urine are measured with a reagent strip.

Preparing the materials

1) Gather the materials: Ketostix® reagent strips, a clean, dry container, and a timer.
2) Check the manufacturer's expiry date indicated on the reagent strip container. Mark the container with the date it was first opened. It must be discarded **six months** after being opened.
   - Ketostix® reagent strips must be stored at room temperature (between 18ºC and 25ºC).
3) Collect a **fresh** urine sample for analysis:
   - empty the bladder completely and discard the urine;
   - drink one or two glasses of water;
   - urinate into a clean, dry container.
4) Take a reagent strip from the container and close the cover **immediately**.
   - Compare the reagent strip with the colour chart on the container to ensure that the strip has not changed colour, which could give a false result.

Testing the urine sample with the reagent strip

1) Dip the reactive part of the strip into the fresh urine sample and remove it right away.
2) Tap the excess fluid off the strip on the edge of the container and start the timer.

Reading and entering the results

1) After **exactly 15 seconds**, place the reagent strip next to the colour chart on the strip container and compare the result under a bright light.

2) Enter the result in your glucose self-monitoring logbook.

Negative	Trace	Small	Moderate	Large
0	0.5 mmol/L	1.5 mmol/L	4 mmol/L	8 mmol/L to 16 mmol/L

Reagent strips that simultaneously measure glucose and ketone bodies in the urine (e.g., Keto-Diastix®, Chemstrip® u G/K) are also available.

7. How is the level of ketone bodies measured from a fingertip blood sample?

Ketone bodies in the blood are measured with a ketone meter.

Preparing the materials

1) Gather the materials: Precision Xtra® meter (to measure blood glucose and ketone bodies), reagent strips for measuring ketosis (ketone bodies), lancing device, lancet.
2) Check the expiry date on the reagent strip envelope.
3) Insert the ketone calibrator into the Precision Xtra® meter. The code on the screen must match the code on the strip.
4) Insert the ketone strip into the Precision Xtra® meter.

Applying the blood sample to the reagent strip

1) Prick the fingertip with the lancing device.
2) Apply a drop of blood to the sensitive area of the strip.

Reading and entering the result

1) Wait for the result to appear on the screen; it should appear within 10 seconds.
2) Write down the result in the self-monitoring logbook.

Negative	Trace	Small	Moderate	Large
0	Less than 0.6 mmol/L	0.6 mmol/L to 1.5 mmol/L	1.5 mmol/L to 3 mmol/L	Over 3 mmol/L

Eating Well

1. Why is it important for people with diabetes to eat well?

Eating well, along with exercising regularly and not smoking, is part of a wholesome routine to promote good health and control the disease more effectively.

There are no "forbidden foods" and there is no "diabetic diet". Instead, the focus is on choosing foods wisely and managing serving/portion size. The diet of a person with diabetes should be satisfying, varied and balanced, not restrictive or punitive.

A treatment regimen can consist solely of a dietary plan or include oral antidiabetic drugs or insulin as well. Either way, healthy eating is essential.

2. Why is it particularly important for people with diabetes to eat well?

Eating well offers a number of advantages for a person with diabetes. A healthy diet:
1) promotes better control of:
    o   blood glucose;
    o   weight;
    o   blood pressure;
    o   fat (lipid) levels in blood;
2) satisfies the body's energy, vitamin and mineral requirements;
3) promotes well-being.

3. What does "eating well" mean for a person with diabetes?

Eating well means choosing **quality foods**, such as those mentioned in *Canada's Food Guide*:

1) Eat at least one dark green and one orange vegetable every day; choose fresh vegetables or fruit over juice.
2) Eat at least half of the recommended grain products in the form of whole grains;
3) Drink skim, 1% or 2% milk or enriched soya beverages every day;
4) Eat meat alternatives such as legumes and tofu often;
5) Eat at least two portions of fish per week;
6) Eat a small amount of good fats (such as olive oil or canola oil) every day;
7) Drink water to quench your thirst.

Eating well also means choosing the **right quantity** for your energy needs. That means eating to satisfy your hunger…but no more.[1]

Some people have trouble recognizing and listening to the body's signals of hunger and satiety (fullness). Hunger can reveal many kinds of needs. It can be physiological, when the body needs energy in the form of nutrients (carbohydrates, proteins and fats) or vitamins and minerals. It can also be psychological, as a way of dealing with stress or negative thoughts or emotional states.

4.　How can a person eat to satisfy hunger… but no more?
Eating to satisfy hunger but not going beyond that point requires moderation. This is the best way of avoiding the ravages associated with dieting or binging on food, both of which are bad for the health.[1]

5.　Practically speaking, how is moderation achieved?
To achieve moderation, it is first necessary to become aware of your body and learn the difference between physiological hunger and psychological hunger. The former is the body's need for nourishment (a need for energy and certain nutrients), while the latter is a defence mechanism, a desire to eat as a way of dealing with uncontrollable emotions, either negative or positive. Being able to make the distinction between these two types of hunger is indispensable to eating the proper amount—that is, neither too much nor too little, but just enough.

---

1. G. Apfeldorfer, *Maigrir, c'est fou* (Éditions Odile Jacob, 2000), 301 pages.

Second, it is necessary to be able to recognize the feeling of being full, that turning point between the pleasure of eating and satiety, when the body has eaten enough to fulfil the body's needs.[2] This task requires constant effort, practice and perseverance.

6.   How can I tell if I have eaten enough?

The following ten suggestions can help you know when you have eaten enough.[2]

1)   **Feel your hunger:** try to eat nothing for four hours. This will help you rediscover the feeling of being hungry and re-establish a healthy relationship with food.

2)   **Establish a routine:** have a similar breakfast every morning and eat meals at regular hours. This will help you feel hungry just before mealtime and then feel full after eating.

3)   **Concentrate on the taste:** pay particular attention, taking small bites and chewing well, to savour the food.

4)   **Slow down:** stretch out your meals to at least 20 minutes. This will help give the body's signals of hunger and satiety time to reach the brain. Putting your knife and fork down between each bite also helps slow down meals.

5)   **Take a break in the middle of the meal:** this will give you a chance to assess whether you are still hungry or whether you have eaten enough. If eating has become less enjoyable, you have eaten enough;

6)   **Avoid distractions:** just eat. Do not read the newspaper, watch television, or carry on an animated conversation. It may be helpful to take frequent breaks during the meal to talk or listen to ensure that you do only one thing at a time.

7)   **Identify your cravings:** ask yourself whether your appetite is triggered by something besides a physiological need or a real hunger. If it is just a craving, take the time to figure out what emotions you are feeling at the time and write them down in a journal.

8)   **Do not overeat now for the future:** wanting to stockpile "just in case" and the fear of "missing out" on food later are frequent consequences of dieting. Come back to the present, and ask yourself how hungry you are right now.

9)   **Be your own judge:** stay tuned in to your own needs instead of eating to please someone else or not to give offence. This will ensure that you are the one who chooses how much you eat.

---

2. Collectif 2007, "Retrouver le plaisir de manger", *Psychologies*, Special issue.

10) **Practice moderation:** eating "just enough" can be done by eating more slowly to better savour the food, reducing portion size, consciously evaluating your hunger throughout the meal, and reducing the number of courses in one meal.

7. How can eating well help a person with diabetes manage blood glucose?

Of all the food groups, carbohydrates have the greatest influence on blood glucose levels. A person with diabetes will maintain better control over blood glucose if:

1) meals are taken at regular hours, at the same time every day. This is particularly true for people with diabetes taking oral antidiabetic drugs that stimulate insulin secretion (for example, Diaβeta®) and those taking insulin. Large variations in blood glucose levels such as hyperglycemia or hypoglycemia can also be diminished;

2) nutrients are spread out evenly over at least three meals, spaced four to six hours apart;

3) carbohydrates are spread out evenly over three meals instead of being consumed once a day (such as in the evening meal);

4) the amount of carbohydrates in meals (and, if necessary, between meals) is moderate and corresponds to the person's energy needs. Carbohydrates are essential, but too many can hamper proper blood glucose management;

5) no meal is skipped;

6) the carbohydrate content of each meal is consistent from one day to the next.

8. How can eating well help control weight?

Eating well can help some people lose weight when they **eat just enough to satisfy their hunger and choose foods containing fewer calories more often.**

For people who are overweight, losing between 5% and 10% of their weight may be enough to improve their control of blood glucose levels, blood pressure and fat levels in the blood.

9. How can eating well help control fat levels in blood?

Choosing **leaner foods** containing higher quality fats can help control fat levels in blood. High fat levels in the blood increase the risk of cardiovascular diseases.

10. How can eating well help manage blood pressure?

Choose a diet rich in:

- o   fruits and vegetables;
- o   skimmed or partly skimmed dairy products;
- o   soluble dietary fibre, found in legumes, oatmeal and oat bran;
- o   whole grains;
- o   vegetable protein, low in saturated fats and cholesterol, as found in legumes and tofu.

This can help reduce blood pressure. These foods generally contain less salt than processed foods that are canned or preserved. Fresh fruits and vegetables also contain potassium, which helps lower blood pressure.

Alcohol should be consumed in moderation, following the Canadian low-risk drinking guidelines:

HEALTHY ADULTS SHOULD LIMIT ALCOHOL CONSUMPTION TO A MAXIMUM OF 2 DRINKS A DAY
o   Men: a maximum of 14 drinks a week
o   Women: a maximum of 9 drinks a week

11. Can a person with diabetes still take pleasure in eating?

Some people, after being diagnosed with diabetes, might have trouble believing that eating will ever be a source of pleasure again. But getting the most out of eating means involving all of your senses, from meal planning, through preparation, to the final enjoyment of the food.

Taking the time to consult cookbooks, choosing the recipes and planning an imaginative meal are all ways of enhancing the pleasure of eating. Markets display an array of colourful and aromatic foods and can also present an opportunity to discuss flavours, aromas and recipes with other food lovers. Preparing meals alone or with others can be a simple task but still provide a chance to experiment with a variety of new flavours and sensations.

Attractive food presentation and an inviting table can also help maximize the pleasure of a delicious and healthy meal.

12. Does eating well mean avoiding cold cuts, French fries, chips and pastries?

These foods can be part of a healthy diet. While it is true that they are often high in fat, sugar and calories, excluding them from your diet altogether is an error, especially if you want to lose weight. It is said that excessive or complete deprivation of a certain food merely increases the desire for it and leads to overindulgence. It is therefore better to give yourself permission to enjoy a few chips once in a while, instead of developing an uncontrollable craving and eating an entire bag. Therefore, these foods play a small role in a balanced diet and can be eaten on occasion, simply for the pleasure they may give.[3]

13. What are some ways to develop better nutritional habits?

Here are some suggestions for improving your eating habits:
1) Set clear, measurable and realistic goals.
2) Go about it gradually, one modification at a time. Small changes can make a big difference.
3) Follow the meal plan created with the help of a dietician.
4) Be sure that you like the food you choose; being satisfied is the best way to prevent slips.
5) Replace food rewards with other treats. For example, buy a book or a CD or take a relaxing bath to pamper yourself.

14. What is a meal plan?

A meal plan is a personalized guide that is prepared by a dietician for a person with diabetes who wants to eat well. It encourages a varied diet of nutritious foods from all the different food groups, suggests quantities, and adheres to dietary recommendations for maintaining good health. It takes into consideration the drugs taken for the treatment of diabetes and other ailments associated with the disease.

---

3. Groupe Équilibre : www.equilibre.ca

The meal plan is built around the seven food groups:
- o   starches;
- o   fruits;
- o   vegetables;
- o   milk and alternatives;
- o   meats and alternatives;
- o   fats;
- o   other choices.

It suggests the **quantities or servings** appropriate to the individual's energy needs. It specifies the recommended carbohydrate content for each meal and snack, as well as the number of servings of meat and alternatives and fats.

The plan can be used as a template for your daily meals. It helps standardize the quantities and servings of food eaten from one day to the next, promoting better control of blood glucose levels while allowing room for a varied diet.

15. Are snacks necessary?

Snacking is not routinely necessary, but having snacks in your meal plan can help spread the carbohydrates out evenly over the course of a day, to better correspond with actual energy (or calorie) needs.

People who inject insulin are sometimes advised to have a snack containing carbohydrates at night, as close as possible to bedtime.

How to Recognize Carbohydrates

1. Why is it necessary to know how to recognize carbohydrates?

The amount of dietary carbohydrates consumed in a meal plays an important role in the increase of blood glucose after the meal. Keeping a watchful eye on the amount of carbohydrates consumed in meals and snacks can improve metabolic control.

2. Carbohydrates can raise blood glucose levels. Should they still be eaten?

Even though they can raise blood glucose, foods containing carbohydrates are essential at every meal. Dietary carbohydrates should provide approximately half of a person's daily energy needs. For example, if a person needs 1800 calories per day, half (900 calories) should come from carbohydrates.

3. What are dietary carbohydrates?

Digested dietary carbohydrates, which can be stored in the liver and muscles, are one of the body's main sources of fuel. Most of the carbohydrates we consume are from plants, which absorb energy from the sun and store it in the form of carbohydrates.

The main types of dietary carbohydrates are glucose, fructose, saccharose (sucrose), lactose, starch, dietary fibre and polyols (or sugar alcohols).

4. What information about carbohydrate content is listed on prepackaged food labels?

Prepackaged food labels list carbohydrate content in grams per portion specified. Carbohydrate content includes sugars, dietary fibre, starches, polyols (or sugar alcohols) and polydextrose.

- o The term "sugars" refers to glucose, fructose, saccharose (sucrose) and lactose. They may be naturally present or added to the product.
- o The term polyols (or sugar alcohols) refers to sugars such as maltitol, mannitol and sorbitol.

5. Which foods contain carbohydrates?

Essentially, there are four food groups that contain carbohydrates: **starchy foods, fruits, vegetables** and **milk**.

Starchy foods contain primarily starches, while fruit and vegetables contain fructose and milk contains lactose. Foods from these groups may also naturally contain glucose and sucrose.

6. How are meals planned for people with diabetes?

There are different meal-planning approaches. The most common are the following
1) The exchange system:

This system involves grouping foods according to their nutritional content (protein, carbohydrates and fats). All the foods within the same group have the same nutritional content, and single portions of food within the same group are known as exchanges or equivalents.

Foods within the same group are interchangeable, as long as the same number of exchanges per meal is consumed. Carbohydrate-containing foods from the starches, fruits, and milk and alternatives groups may also be interchanged to ensure a varied diet.

This system categorizes food into seven main groups:
- o Starches
- o Fruits

- o Vegetables
- o Milk and alternatives
- o Other choices
- o Meat and alternatives
- o Fats

An eighth group of "low calorie foods" has recently been added. There are no restrictions on the consumption of foods in this group, given their negligible effect on blood glucose and blood lipids.

Each exchange contains on average 15 g of carbohydrates or 3 teaspoons of sugar, except for vegetables, meat, and fats. One exchange of vegetables contains an average of 5 g of carbohydrates or 1 teaspoon of sugar. Most raw and cooked vegetables contain few carbohydrates and therefore have little effect on blood glucose. Vegetables with the highest carbohydrate content are included in the starches group, which do have an effect on blood glucose.

A few examples of exchanges:

Foods	One serving corresponding to one exchange (15 g of carbohydrates or 3 teaspoons of sugar)
Starches	
Bread	1 slice (30 g serving)
Cooked spaghetti	75 mL (1/3 cup)
Lentils	125 mL (1/2 cup)
Sweet peas	250 mL (1 cup)
Fruits	
Banana	½ large (90 g serving)
Kiwi	2 small
Orange juice	125 mL (½ cup)
Milk and alternatives	
Milk	250 mL (1 cup)
Plain yogurt	175 mL (¾ cup)

The exchange system is used mainly to plan meals for people with diabetes whose treatment includes diet, oral antidiabetic drugs or fixed-dose insulin.

This system is used by Diabetes Québec and a detailed explanation is provided in the brochure entitled *Meal Planning for People with Diabetes.*[1] It is also used by the American Diabetes Association (ADA). The system recommended by the Canadian Diabetes Association (CDA), which has recently been revised, closely resembles the one used by Diabetes Québec and the ADA. It is outlined in a new guide entitled *Beyond the Basics: Meal Planning for Healthy Eating, Diabetes Prevention and Management.*[2]

AMOUNT OF CARBOHYDRATES IN ONE EXCHANGE		
Food groups	**Systems**	
DQ/CDA	**DQ and ADA**	**CDA**
Starches/Grains and Starches	15 g	15 g
Fruits	15 g	15 g
Vegetables	0 g to 5 g	–
Milk /Milk and Alternatives	12 g to 15 g	15 g
Other choices	15 g	15 g
Meat and Alternatives	0 g	0 g
Fats	0 g	0 g
Low calorie foods /Extras	< 5 g	< 5 g

2) Basic carbohydrate counting
    This method involves predetermining the grams of carbohydrates to be contained in each meal and snack.
    Basic carbohydrate counting can be used by anyone with diabetes and is especially useful for people who have trouble using the food exchange system.
3) Advanced carbohydrate counting
    Advanced carbohydrate counting involves counting the total number of carbohydrates from all meals as precisely as possible.

---

1. http://www.diabete.qc.ca/english/publications/pdf/meal_planning.pdf (updated version due in 2008).
2. http://www.diabetes.ca/section_about/btb2006.asp.

This method is particularly useful for people with diabetes who inject insulin according to a varied carbohydrate intake.

The amount of insulin for each meal is calculated using an insulin: carbohydrate ratio (that is, a number of units of insulin for every 10 g of carbohydrates). The insulin dose is thus proportionate to the amount of carbohydrates consumed.

The doctor first determines the insulin: carbohydrate ratio specific to a person. The ratio can also be done with the help of a dietary journal detailing the amount of carbohydrates consumed at every meal, the amount of insulin injected, and blood glucose readings. The ratio may differ from one meal to another over the course of the same day.

Advanced carbohydrate counting allows for a certain amount of flexibility, since it does not require planning the specific amount of carbohydrates for every meal and snack.

7. Can foods such as pastries, jams, and soft drinks be included in meals?

These foods fall under the "other choices" category in the guide *Meal Planning for People with Diabetes* and may be substituted for an equal quantity of carbohydrates in any other food.

Foods containing fewer than 3 g of carbohydrates per serving do not need to be counted in the meal's carbohydrate total, provided they are eaten one serving at a time.

For example:
The 2.5 g of carbohydrates contained in 10 ml or 2 teaspoons of light fruit jam are generally not added to the total breakfast carbohydrates.

Foods containing more than 3 g of carbohydrate per serving may be eaten as part of a meal and their carbohydrate content must be counted.

Pastries, pies, cookies, ice cream, chocolate, chips and crackers contain not only carbohydrates but also fats. These foods should be consumed only occasionally and in moderation because their high calorie content can cause weight gain.

8. Where can information on the carbohydrate content of specific foods be found?

There are several ways to find out about the carbohydrate content of the foods we consume.

1) **Product labels:**
Nutritional value is printed on food packaging.

2) **Food composition tables:**
Health Canada publishes a useful table entitled "Nutrient Value of Some Common Foods" (2008). It is available in bookstores and on the Health Canada website.[3]

3) **Nutritional information provided by restaurants:**
Some restaurants provide nutritional information about the food they serve. Be sure to ask.

4) **Cookbooks:**
Many cookbooks list the nutritional value of their recipes.

5) **Food exchange lists:**
A dietician can provide a list of food exchanges. The lists published by the Ministère de la Santé et des Services sociaux and Diabetes Québec (*Meal Planning for People with Diabetes*) and by the Canadian Diabetes Association (*Beyond the Basics: Meal Planning for Eating, Diabetes Prevention and Management*) are also available for consultation.

6) **Carbohydrate factors:**
The carbohydrate factor is the amount of carbohydrates contained in 1 g of a given food.

For example:
a 100 g pear with a carbohydrate factor of 0.12 contains 12 g total carbohydrates:
100 g x 0.12 = 12 g of carbohydrates

A table of carbohydrate factors can be found in the book "Pumping Insulin".[4]

3. http://www.hc-sc.gc.ca/fn-an/alt_formats/hpfb-dgpsa/pdf/nutrition/nvscf-vnqau_e.pdf.
4. Walsh John and Ruth Roberts, *Pumping Insulin*, 4th ed. (Torrey Pines Press, 2006).

9. What amount of carbohydrates should be eaten daily?

Total daily carbohydrate intake is determined by energy (or caloric) needs, which are evaluated according to a person's size, weight, sex, age and the amount of physical activity he or she engages in.

On average, carbohydrates should provide half of a person's caloric needs. The rest should be supplied by proteins, fats and alcohol.

To maintain adequate body function, a person should consume more than 130 g of carbohydrates a day. Generally, for an adolescent or an adult with diabetes, the amount should fall between 200 g and 300 g per day, or at least:
- o 6 exchanges of starches and
- o 3 exchanges of fruits and
- o 4 exchanges of vegetables and
- o 2 exchanges of milk and alternatives and
- o 6 exchanges of meat and alternatives and
- o approximately 4 exchanges of fats and
- o occasionally, 1 exchange of other choices

This corresponds to at least 60 g of carbohydrates per meal.

10. Should the same quantity of carbohydrates be eaten every day?

It depends on the individual's treatment regimen.

1) **People with diabetes whose treatment consists solely of a dietary regimen or of a diet combined with a fixed medical treatment** (either oral antidiabetic drugs or insulin) should eat the same quantity of carbohydrates at every meal and schedule meals at regular times.

   The total carbohydrate amount should be spread out over the course of the day. This will help avoid a spike in blood glucose after meals.

2) **People who count carbohydrates and inject insulin according to the amount of carbohydrates ingested** may vary their carbohydrate consumption from one day to another. Eating balanced meals should remain a priority, however, because it is vital to good health and because overeating can lead to weight gain.

11. What is the glycemic index?

According to the CDA, the glycemic index is a scale ranking carbohydrate-rich foods by their tendency to raise blood glucose levels after consumption compared to a standard food (glucose or white bread).

Low glycemic index foods, such as dried beans, cause blood glucose to rise more gradually than high glycemic index foods, such as white bread or mashed potatoes. Some low glycemic index foods:

- milled or stone ground whole grains,
- oatmeal,
- barley,
- pasta,
- legumes,
- sweet potato.[5]

It has been found that taking the glycemic index of food into account when planning meals brings an additional benefit to carbohydrate counting. Low glycemic index foods are said to help control blood glucose levels after meals. Although studies are contradictory, it appears that the fibre in these foods may positively influence insulin sensitivity and even pancreatic function.

12. Why should fibre-rich foods be part of the diet of a person with diabetes?

Fibres are a form of carbohydrate. They resist digestion by human enzymes and are therefore not broken down in the small intestine. As a result, they arrive in the large intestine intact and do not raise blood glucose levels.

Some sources of fibre
Fruits
Whole grains
Vegetables
Legumes
Nuts
Oat and wheat bran

5. See http://www.diabetes.ca/files/Diabetes_GL_FINAL2_CPG03.pdf.

Eating a wide variety of fibre-rich foods is recommended, since they are also a good source of vitamins and minerals. Such foods should be introduced gradually to avoid unpleasant effects such as bloating and flatulence. It is also important to drink a sufficient amount of liquid to ensure that the fibres perform their function efficiently. The target amount of fibres for people with diabetes is the same as it is for the general population, namely, between 21 g and 38 g per day, depending on sex.

Moreover, fibres help:
1) **control blood glucose:** very large amounts of fibres (50 g/day) can help control blood glucose in some people with diabetes;
2) **avoid constipation:** fibres improve intestinal transit by increasing stool volume; fibres promote a healthy colon (large intestine);
3) **control blood cholesterol:** large amounts of fibres help lower blood cholesterol in some people with diabetes;
4) **control weight:** foods rich in fibre are low in calories but still leave you feeling full.

Fats:
Making the Right Choices

1. Why should people with diabetes limit their fat consumption?

People with diabetes have a serious risk of developing cardiovascular disease. If they also have elevated levels of triglycerides and bad cholesterol in their blood, the risk is even higher.

Limiting consumption of certain fats such as saturated and trans fats helps control blood lipids, also known as blood fats. The main types of blood lipids are:
  - triglycerides;
  - total cholesterol;
  - HDL-cholesterol (good cholesterol);
  - LDL-cholesterol (bad cholesterol).

Limiting fat consumption also helps control weight.

2. Why does fat consumption lead to weight gain?

One gram of carbohydrate or protein contains four calories, while one gram of fat contains nine calories, more than double.

  - 5 mL or 1 teaspoon of sugar (5 g of carbohydrates) contains 20 calories;
  - 5 mL or 1 teaspoon of oil (5 g of fat) contains about 45 calories.

3. If fats can be bad for the health, why is it necessary to eat them?

Fats are part of a balanced diet, just like carbohydrates and proteins. They are an excellent source of energy. They contain essential fatty acids, which help make up certain vitamins and hormones, and play a vital role in the body.

4. What is the recommended daily fat consumption for a healthy diet?

It is recommended that less than 35% of a person's daily calories should be ingested in the form of fats:

- less than 7% of calories from saturated fats and limited intake of trans fats;
- less than 10% of calories from polyunsaturated fats;
- higher intake of omega-3 from fish and vegetable sources;
- more frequent substitution of saturated by monounsaturated fats.

5. Should people with diabetes count fats the way they count carbohydrates?

Not necessarily. In most cases, there are other ways (eating smaller portions of meat or choosing lower fat cheeses, for example) to reduce the amount of dietary fat to a satisfactory level. It should help to remember that people usually eat large quantities of fat on impulse because it adds flavour, making the food more appealing.

6. Which foods contain fats?

The following foods contain either visible or hidden fats:

Visible fats
Oils
Butter
Margarine
Lard
Lard
Vegetable fats
Meats

Hidden fats
Meats and cold cuts
Fatty fish (mackerel and herring, among others)
Sauces (such as mayonnaise or béarnaise, white or cheese sauce)
Some types of prepared dishes
Nuts and seeds
Avocado
Cookies, pastries, croissants, brioches

7. Which fats are found naturally in foods?

The following types of fats occur naturally:

1) saturated fats, usually of animal origin;
2) cholesterol, always of animal origin;
3) unsaturated fats, primarily of vegetable origin (monounsaturated and polyunsaturated);
4) Trans fats, naturally present in small quantities in meats and dairy products.

No food contains only one type of fat. They are classified according to the predominant fat source.

For example:
Sunflower oil, very high in polyunsaturated fats, also contains small quantities of saturated and monounsaturated fats. It is classified as a source of polyunsaturated fats.

8. What are trans or hydrogenated fats?

These fats are produced by the food industry and do not occur naturally. They are made from oils that are processed to transform them from a liquid to a solid state. Examples include partially hydrogenated margarine, vegetable fats and fats used in bakery products.

Regular consumption of these fats increases the risk of cardiovascular disease because they are metabolized in the same way as saturated fats.

In June 2007, Health Canada adopted the recommendations of a working group that recommended reducing the trans fat content of foods. The food industry has two years to limit trans fat content to:

○ 2% of the total amount of fat in oils and soft margarines;
○ 5% of other foods, including prepared ingredients or ingredients sold in restaurants.

9. Why do we have to choose fats carefully?

Some people are predisposed to abnormally high fat levels in their blood. In such cases, different types of fats and the foods that contain them can have either beneficial or harmful effects.

Harmful effects:

	Triglycerides	Total Cholesterol	HDL Cholesterol	LDL Cholesterol
Cholesterol		↑		↑
Saturated fats		↑	↓	↑
Trans or hydrogenated fats		↑	↓	↑

↑ increase   ↓ decrease

Beneficial effects:

	Triglycerides	Total Cholesterol	HDL Cholesterol	LDL Cholesterol
Monounsaturated fats	=	↓	↑ OR =	↓
Polyunsaturated omega-3 fats	↓ OR =	=	↑ OR =	↑ OR =

↑ increase   ↓ decrease   = no change

Some types of fat are better for your heart and blood vessels than others. Foods containing **monounsaturated and polyunsaturated** fats should be preferred over anything containing saturated fats, trans or hydrogenated fats, or cholesterol.

10. Which foods contain which types of fat?

SATURATED FATS	
Animal origin*	**Vegetable origin**
Butter	Coconut or copra oil
Cream, ice cream	Palm oil
Yogurt 8% M.F.	Palm kernel oil
Cheeses	Coconut
Whole milk 3.25 % M.F.	
Lard	
Eggs	
Tallow	
Meats	
Poultry and poultry skin	

* These also contain cholesterol.

UNSATURATED FATS	
Monounsaturated	**Polyunsaturated**
Almonds	Pumpkin seeds
Peanuts	Linseed
Avocado	Sunflower seeds
Sesame seeds	Borage oil
Peanut oil	Safflower oil
Canola oil	Pumpkin oil
Olive oil	Linseed oil
Hazelnut oil	Corn oil
Sesame oil	Walnut oil
Hazelnuts	Grapeseed oil
Cashew nuts	Soya oil
Brazil nuts	Sunflower oil
Olives	Evening primrose oil
Pecans	Walnuts
Pistachios	Pine nuts
	Fatty fish (e.g., salmon, mackerel)

UNSATURATED FATS MONOUNSATURATED AND POLYUNSATURATED
Soft non-hydrogenated margarine (e.g. Becel®, Crystal®, Lactantia®, Nuvel®, Olivina®, etc.)

TRANS OR HYDROGENATED FATS (VEGETABLE ORIGIN)	
Hydrogenated vegetable oil	Soft margarine
Hard margarine	Vegetable oil shortening
Certain bakery products	Fast food
Snacks	

11. How can the consumption of fats, and trans or hydrogenated fats in particular, be reduced?

It is useful to remember that:

1) all fats have comparable energy value: 5 mL or 1 teaspoon of oil, butter or margarine all contain 40 to 45 calories;

2) no oil is low-fat, even if it is called "light".

To eat less fat, do the following:

1) develop the habit of measuring fats with a teaspoon or tablespoon; one teaspoon equals 5 mL and one tablespoon equals 15 mL;*

2) choose leaner cuts of meat (10% or less of fat), poultry, fish, molluscs, and crustaceans on occasion; trim visible fat and remove skin before cooking;

3) eat reasonably sized servings of meat or alternatives, no bigger than the palm of your hand; a meat serving that size equals 90 g (3 oz) of meat;

4) eat fish more often, at least two or three times a week;

5) incorporate dishes with legumes (beans, etc.) into your meals;

6) eat less cheese or select leaner cheeses more often; leaner choices include unripened cheeses (for example, cottage, quark, goat's and cow's milk cheese). Cheese with over 20% fat content has two or three times more fat than meat;

7) drink partially skimmed or skimmed milk (1% m.f. or 2% m.f.) instead of whole milk (3.25% m.f.);

8) reduce daily consumption of fatty foods like butter and cream sauces, pastries, prepackaged muffins, croissants, brioches, cookies, and so on. Save these foods for special occasions only. Replace them with yogurt, mousses, skim or partially skim milk desserts, puddings, soy mousses, dry cookies, homemade muffins and dessert breads, etc.

12. Which cooking methods can lower fat content?

When cooking, use methods requiring the least amount of fat possible.

---

* One tablespoon equals three teaspoons.

Cooking method	Foods
Water	Boiled beef, boiled chicken
Steam	Vegetables, fish, pressure-cooked or steamed rice
Conventional oven or microwave	Poultry, roasts (beef, chicken, veal), fish, fruits, gratin with light béchamel
Double-boiler	Scrambled eggs
Braising	Mixed plate cooked in clay pot or pressure cooker
Grill	Cast-iron, oven or BBQ grill: meats, poultry, vegetables, higher-fat fish such as salmon
Frying	Non-stick frying pan for eggs, omelettes and sliced meats
Closed packet	Fish, lean meats, potatoes, fruits
Simmering or stewing	Stewing meats
Gros sel[2]	Fish, chicken

13. Can some foods help lower blood fat levels?

Yes, it appears that some food components can lower blood fat. Vegetable phytosterols, omega-3 fatty acids and soluble fibre are the most well known.

1) **Vegetable phytosterols** (or sterols/stanols) have a beneficial effect on blood fat levels, primarily on total cholesterol and LDL or bad cholesterol. They are believed to prevent the absorption of cholesterol in the intestine, thereby reducing the amount of bad cholesterol in the blood. The recommended daily consumption is 2 to 3 grams of vegetable sterols, which are found primarily in vegetable oils, nuts, seeds, and whole grains, but only in very small quantities. Because huge quantities of these foods would have to be consumed in order to have an effect, sterols/stanols are marketed as supplements and added to certain foods (not sold in Canada).

2) **Omega-3 fatty acids** help protect against cardiovascular disease. Among other things, they help reduce blood triglyceride and cholesterol.

---

2. Heat the gros sel (coarse sea salt) in the oven between two aluminum plates for approximately 30 minutes at 500°F (260°C). Remove from the oven and place the chicken or fish in the salt. Allow to cook 30 minutes at 350°F (175°C).

They are found in:

o   foods of both vegetable origin, such as canola oil, linseed oil, and linseed (alphalinolenic or ALN acid);

o   foods of animal origin, such as fish and fish oil (DHA and EPA).

The most significant effects on cardiac health have been observed with omega-3 of fish origin.

The protective effects of omega-3 fatty acids from fish have led to recommendations for the general population and people with diabetes in particular to eat fish two or three times a week. As for omega-3 fatty acids of vegetable origin, the recommended daily intake is the following: 1 g of ALN for women and 1.6 g for men.

The following chart presents a few examples of food sources of omega-3 fatty acids:

Foods	Total amount (g)	ALN	EPA	DHA
Natrel® omega-3 milk beverage, 1% or 2% M.F. (250 mL or 1 cup)	0.30	0.30	0.00	0.00
Naturegg® Break-Free Omega 3 liquid eggs (50 mL)	0.32	0.03	0.15	0.14
Naturegg® Omega 3 shell eggs* (50 g or 1 unit)	0.40	0.31	0.01	0.08
Becel Omega3plus® margarine (10 g or 2 tsp)	0.60	0.55	0.05	
Soya oil (15 mL or 3 tsp)	0.94	0.94	0.00	0.00
Canola oil (15 mL or 3 tsp)	1.32	1.32	0.00	0.00
Linseed oil (15 mL or 3 tsp.)	7.74	7.74	0.00	0.00
Chopped walnuts (60 mL or 30 g)	2.69	2.69	0.00	0.00
Ground linseed (10 mL or 2 tsp)	1.09	1.09	0.00	0.00
Salba** (30 mL or 2 tbsp)	2.45	2.45	0.00	0.00

Foods	Total amount (g)	ALN	EPA	DHA
Cooked wild or farmed rainbow trout (75 g or 2 ½ oz)	0.93	0.06	0.25	0.62
Baked or broiled blue mackerel (75 g or 2 ½ oz)	0.99	0.09	0.38	0.52
Baked or grilled fresh red tuna (75 g or 2 ½ oz)	1.13	0.00	0.27	0.86
Canned white tuna, in water (75 g or 2 ½ oz)	0.70	0.05	0.18	0.47
Atlantic sardines, in oil, drained, with bones (75 g or 2 ½ oz)	1.11	0.37	0.36	0.38
Baked or broiled Atlantic herring (75 g or 2 ½ oz)	1.61	0.10	0.68	0.83
Atlantic herring, smoked and salted (75 g or 2 ½ oz)	1.72	0.11	0.73	0.88
Canned pink salmon, drained, with bones, salted (75 g or 2 ½ oz)	0.84	0.05	0.27	0.52
Canned keta salmon, drained, with bones, salted (75 g or 2 ½ oz)	0.93	0.04	0.36	0.53
Canned sockeye salmon, drained, with bones, salted (75 g or 2 ½ oz)	1.46	0.07	0.55	0.84
Cooked Atlantic salmon (75 g or 2 ½ oz)	1.70	0.09	0.52	1.09
Quinnat salmon, smoked (75 g or 2 ½ oz)	0.34	0.00	0.14	0.20

3) **Soluble fibres** also have a beneficial effect on bad cholesterol. The recommended daily intake is 10 g to 25 g. Soluble fibres are often part of a low-saturated fat and cholesterol diet, in combination with drug therapy.

---

* Eggs from hens raised on linseed feed
** Grain high in omega-3 fatty acids and antioxidants

The following foods provide 3 g of soluble fibres per serving:

Food	Amount
All-Bran Buds®	75 mL (⅓ cup)
Psyllium husks or powder	5 mL (1 tsp)
Metamucil®	15 mL (1 tbsp)
Cooked oat bran or porridge	250 mL (1 cup)
Red kidney beans	125 mL (½ cup)
Ground linseed	75 mL (⅓ cup)
Roasted soy seeds	75 mL (⅓ cup)
Canned artichoke hearts	2

14. Are there other ways to lower blood fat levels?

The following factors can help control fat levels in blood:

	Triglycerides	Total cholesterol	HDL Cholesterol	LDL Cholesterol
Increasing physical activity	↓	↓	↑ OR =	↓
Losing weight	↓			
Quitting smoking*	↓	↓	↑	↓

↓ decreases   ↑ increases   = no change

---

*   The effects of smoking on blood fats that have been observed may be linked to other factors associated with quitting smoking.

How to Read Food Labels

1. What information is listed on prepackaged food labels?

The following nutritional information is found on prepackaged food labels:

1) the Nutrition Facts table;
2) the list of ingredients;
3) the product's nutritional and health claims.

Health Canada regulates food labelling in Canada through the *Food and Drugs Act*. This labelling statute was updated and its final version published on January 1, 2003. Since December 2007, nutritional labelling has been mandatory on all prepackaged foods. The Canadian Food Inspection Agency (CFIA) is charged with protecting the public against fraud or misrepresentation*.

2. What information is listed in the Nutrition Facts table?

The Nutrition Facts table on prepackaged food labels provides information about a specified quantity of the food. This information includes:

1) the caloric value of the food in the specified serving;
2) the content of 13 listed nutrients in the specified serving;
3) the percentage of the recommended Daily Value (% DV) represented by that serving.

---

* See the following web sites on food labelling in Canada:
  http://www.hc-sc.gc.ca/fn-an/label-etiquet/nutrition/index_e.html
  http://www.hc-sc.gc.ca/fn-an/label-etiquet/index_e.html

```
┌─────────────────────────────────────────┐
│ Nutrition Facts                         │
│ per 125 mL (87 g)                       │
│ ─────────────────────────────────────── │
│ Amount                    % Daily Value │
│ Calories 80                             │
│ ─────────────────────────────────────── │
│ Fat 0,5 g                         1 %   │
│   Saturated Fat 0 g                     │
│   + trans Fat 0 g                       │
│ Cholesterol 0 mg                        │
│ Sodium 0 mg                       0 %   │
│ Carbohydrate 18 g                 6 %   │
│   Fibre 2 g                       8 %   │
│   Sugars 2 g                            │
│ Protein 3 g                             │
│ ─────────────────────────────────────── │
│ Vitamin A    2 %   Vitamin C   10 %     │
│ Calcium      0 %   Iron         2 %     │
└─────────────────────────────────────────┘
```

3. What information is in the list of ingredients?

The list includes all the food's ingredients presented in decreasing order of weight; in other words, the ingredients present in the greatest amount are listed first.

4. What is important to know about the manufacturer's nutritional claims?

The new nutrient labelling regulation permits two types of nutritional claims:

1) **nutrient content claims**: these are statements or expressions describing the nutritional elements of a food;

2) **health claims**: these include any representation affirming, suggesting or implying a relationship between a food or an ingredient in the food and a health effect.

Nutrient content and health claims are useful for people with diabetes as they enable them to make better-informed nutritional choices.

5.   What type of nutrient content claims appears on labels?

The following chart presents several examples of nutrient content claims on food product labels, along with their meanings.

Claims	Meaning per specified serving
Calories	
"Calorie reduced"	At least 25% fewer calories than the food to which it is compared
"Low calorie"	No more than 40 calories
"Calories free"	Less than 5 calories
Fats	
"Fat free"	Less than 0.5 g of fat
"Low fat"	No more than 3 g of fat
"Low saturated fat"	No more than 2 g of saturated fat and trans fat in total, and no more than 15% of total calories derived from saturated fat and trans fat
"No trans fatty acids"	Less than 0.2 g of trans fatty acids and "low in saturated fats"
Cholesterol	
"Cholesterol free"	Less than 2 mg of cholesterol and low in saturated fat
Carbohydrate and sugar	
"Sugar free"	Less than 0.5 g of sugar
"Reduced sugar"	At least 25% less sugar than the regular version than the food to which it is compared
"No sugar added"	No added sugar such as saccharose, fructose, glucose, molasses, fruit juice, honey, syrup, etc.
Fibre	
"Source of fibre"	2 g or more of fibre
"Good source of fibre"	4 g or more of fibre
"Very good source of fibre"	6 g or more of fibre
Calcium	
"Good source of calcium"	At least 165 mg of calcium

If a manufacturer wants to use the term "light" to describe a product, the label must indicate precisely what in fact makes the product "light". If the term refers to nutritive value, it is authorized only for food products with a reduced amount of **calories** or **fats**.

6. What kinds of health claims are authorized?

For the first time in Canada, manufacturers may include claims regarding diet on a food product. Only claims based on scientifically demonstrated links between the food product and a reduced risk of chronic disease are authorized. Such links include the following:

- o A low-sodium and high-potassium diet may reduce the risk of high blood pressure;
- o A healthy diet with adequate calcium and vitamin D may reduce the risk of osteoporosis;
- o A diet low in saturated and trans fats may reduce the risk of cardiovascular disease;
- o A diet rich in fruits and vegetables may reduce the risk of certain types of cancer.

An example of a health claim:
"A healthy diet including a variety of fruits and vegetables may help reduce the risk of certain types of cancer."

It is also permitted to make claims regarding cavities for candy, gum or breath fresheners, since they contain only minute quantities of carbohydrates that promote tooth decay.

7. How is the law applied?

The Canadian Food Inspection Agency (CFIA)* is in charge of implementing inspections to determine whether nutritional information is in compliance with the regulations enacted by the government in 2003.

---

* www.inspection.gc.ca/english/toce/shtml

8. **What is a sugar substitute?**

    A sugar substitute is a substance that replaces table sugar (saccharose or sucrose) as a food sweetener. Some add calories or carbohydrates and are therefore known as **nutritive** sweeteners; others do not and are called **non-nutritive**. Any calories or carbohydrates added by nutritive sweeteners can affect blood glucose levels to varying degrees and must be calculated in the carbohydrate count or meal plan. Non-nutritive sweeteners have no calories and little effect on blood glucose.

9. **What types of nutritive sugar substitutes are found in prepackaged foods?**

    The following chart presents the various nutritive sugar substitutes that raise blood glucose, along with a few of their properties.

Nutritive sugar substitute	Some properties
Fructose	• Possible effect on blood glucose, triglycerides, cholesterol and weight; • Consumption of more than 60 g per day is not recommended for people with diabetes; • Risk of gastro-intestinal symptoms
Sorbitol Mannitol Xylitol Isomalt Maltitol Erythritol Hydrogenated starch hydrolysate	• Provides fewer calories than sugars because they are only partly absorbed • Glycemic response is weaker than sugars • Do not cause cavities • Risk of gastro-intestinal symptoms due to varying degrees of laxative effect
Lactitol	• Not absorbed; provides calories • No glycemic effect • Risk of gastro-intestinal symptoms due to varying degrees of laxative effect

In the above table, the sugar substitutes ending with "-ol" and hydrogenated starch hydrolysate are also known collectively as "polyols" or "sugar alcohols". They come from plants such as fruits or berries, but they can also be synthetically manufactured.

Compared to table sugar (sucrose), sugar alcohols provide fewer calories and carbohydrates and do not raise blood glucose as much because they are digested more slowly or only partially absorbed by the intestine. Foods that contain nutritive sugar substitutes include gum, candy, chocolate, jam, ice cream, syrup, nutrition bars, and cough drops.

Polydextrose is also a sugar alcohol. This food additive is used primarily to add texture to prepackaged foods. Unlike other sugar alcohols, it does not have a sweet taste. Very little is absorbed, it provides very few calories, and it does not increase blood glucose.

10. What non-nutritive sugar substitutes are authorized in Canada and are found in some prepackaged foods?

The following chart presents the various non-nutritive sugar substitutes that do not increase blood glucose and their properties.

Non-nutritive sugar substitutes	Commercial names and/or foods that contain them	Sources	ADI* mg/kg/ day	Maximum daily consumption** (mg)
Acesulfame-potassium (K)	Not authorized for purchase	• Prepackaged foods or drinks	15	750
Aspartame	Equal® NutraSweet® Sweet'N'Low® Private brands	• Packets, tablets or powders • Prepackaged foods or drinks	40	2000
Cyclamates	Sucaryl® SugarTwin® Sweet'N'Low® Private brands	• Packets, tablets, powder or liquid • Unauthorized in prepackaged food or drink	11***	550
Saccharine	Hermesetas®	• Packets, tablets • Unauthorized in prepackaged foods or drinks	5***	250
Sucralose	Splenda®	• Packets or powder • Prepackaged foods or drinks	9	450
Neotame	–	• Prepackaged foods or drinks	2	100
Thaumatine	Talin®****	• Prepackaged foods	unspecified	–

*   ADI = Acceptable Daily Intake.
**   For a 50-kg (110 lb) adult
*** Not recommended during pregnancy or while breastfeeding
****Not available in retail

Recently, the Natural Health Products Directorate (NHPD) provisionally authorized the use of Stevia and its extracts such as stevioside as a medicinal ingredient and sweetening agent in natural health products. The daily intake for extracts such as stevioside was set at 1 mg/kg/day up to 70 mg and a maximum of 280 mg/day for an adult taking powdered Stevia leaves. Stevia is available in packet, powder or liquid form. Stevia is not recommended by Health Canada for children, pregnant or nursing women, or people with hypotension (low blood pressure).

11. How are sugar alcohols listed in the Nutrition Facts chart on prepackaged foods?

They are listed under total carbohydrates and are often referred to by their specific names or as sugar alcohols.

12. How are carbohydrates that can affect blood glucose measured in products containing sugar alcohols?

Here is an excerpt from a Nutrition Facts table providing information on the carbohydrate content:

Carbohydrate	19 g
Sugars	3 g
Sorbitol	16 g

Despite the notable differences between them, one rule applies to nearly all sugar alcohols. Because only half of them is digested or absorbed, their carbohydrate content must be divided by two and subtracted from the total carbohydrate count.

In the above example, the body will not absorb 8 g of sorbitol. From the total carbohydrate count (19 g), only 11 g of carbohydrates will have any effect on blood glucose:

16 g of sorbitol ÷ 2 = 8 g of carbohydrates not absorbed
19 g total carbohydrates – 8 g of unabsorbed sorbitol = 11 g of carbohydrates

Nonetheless, it is not recommended to match rapid acting insulin to the intake of sugar alcohols.

Because of their physiological properties, lactitol and polydextrose are not absorbed at all and their carbohydrate content should be subtracted in total from the carbohydrate count of the food.

Preparing meals

1. How should people with diabetes go about preparing their meals?

Example: Spaghetti with meat sauce.

Step 1

- o   Refer to the **meal plan**.
- o   In the sample menu, find the recommended number of servings (or choices) of each food group for the appropriate meal.

Example of 75 g of carbohydrate sample menu:

Sample menu	
Lunch	
Starches	3 servings
Fruits	1 serving
Vegetables	2 servings
Milk	1 serving
Meat and alternatives	3 servings
Fats	1 serving

Step 2

- o   Assign the meal chosen to the appropriate food group.

Spaghetti with tomato meat sauce:

- • spaghetti = starches
- • tomato and meat sauce = meats and alternatives, vegetables.

Step 3

o Find the serving size for each type of food.

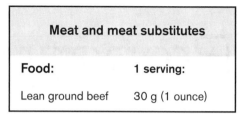

Starch group 1 serving = 15 g of carbohydrates		Meat and meat substitutes	
Food:	**1 serving:**	**Food:**	**1 serving:**
Spaghetti (cooked)	75 mL (¹/₃ cup)	Lean ground beef	30 g (1 ounce)

Step 4

o Figure out how many servings you will eat.
Example:

75 mL (¹/₃ cup) of spaghetti	=	1 serving
Therefore:		
250 mL (1 cup)	=	3 servings
Tomato and meat sauce containing 90 g (3 ounces)	=	3 servings of meat and alternatives, 1 serving of vegetables

In this case, the meal contains all the recommended servings of starches and meat and alternatives, as well as one serving of vegetables. The menu should then be completed with the other food groups (one serving each of milk, vegetables, fruit, and fat).

2. How is the nutritional value of a recipe calculated?

To figure out the nutritional value of a recipe, you need the following information:
1) the number of servings* or units produced by the recipe;
2) the nutritional value, in grams (g), of carbohydrates, proteins and fats provided by one serving or unit of the recipe.

---

* One serving as defined in the recipe does not necessarily correspond to one serving of a food group (for example, one muffin equals one recipe serving, but it also equals two servings of 15 g of carbohydrates, or 30 g per muffin).

Example:

Prune muffins	
Ingredients:	flour, prunes, sugar, oil, eggs, baking soda
Servings or units:	18 muffins
Nutritional value per muffin:	28 g carbohydrate and 5 g fat

3. How is the nutritional value of a recipe adapted to a meal plan?

If the meal plan is divided into 15 g servings of carbohydrates, the number of 15 g servings in the food to be eaten has to be determined. Let us take as an example one prune muffin, from the above recipe.

28 g ÷ 15 g = 1.9 = 2 servings of 15 g

Knowing the meal plan well will help you classify the food according to the correct food groups.

In this example, the prune muffin counts as one fruit serving containing 15 g of carbohydrates and one starch serving containing 15 g of carbohydrates.

The prune muffin also contains 5 g of fat. Since foods from the starch and fruit groups are not sources of fat, there is therefore one serving of fat in this muffin. This must be accounted for in the daily food record.

Fit the muffin into the number of servings in the appropriate meal in your sample menu.

Example of 75 g of carbohydrate sample menu:

Sample menu	
Dinner	
Starches	3 servings
Fruits	1 serving
Vegetables	2 servings
Milk	1 serving
Meat and alternatives	3 servings
Fats	1 serving

In this example, one muffin counts as one serving of fruit, one serving of starch, and one serving of fat. Complete the meal with one serving of milk, two additional servings of starch, three servings of meat and alternatives, and two servings of vegetables.

If the meal plan is divided into fixed amounts of carbohydrates per meal, keep track of the carbohydrate content of the muffins you eat. Complete the menu to reach the recommended carbohydrate content.

4. **What if the serving yield and nutritional value of a recipe are unknown? Is it still possible to figure out the carbohydrate content?**
   Yes. If you do not know the nutritional value of a recipe, it can be calculated from the list of recipe ingredients, using a food composition table. For carbohydrate content, divide the total value by the number of servings (or units) in the recipe.

Special Situations

Eating in Restaurants

1.   Can people with diabetes eat out in restaurants?

Yes. Occasional restaurant dining is one of life's pleasures, and there is no need to eliminate it because of diabetes. People with diabetes have to find ways to enjoy the experience while following the meal plan.

It is still possible to manage blood glucose levels, even if you eat out everyday (for lunch, for example). It is a question of being careful about food choices and amounts. However, remember that the fat content of restaurant food is on average 20% to 25% higher than food prepared at home, and often the meals served are not well balanced. Restaurant food is also generally higher in sodium (salt). These factors must be taken into account.

2.   How should people with diabetes choose a meal from a restaurant menu?

There are several strategies to help people with diabetes choose meals in restaurants.
1)   Know your meal plan.
2)   Find out about the ingredients of the dishes on the menu.
3)   Choose carbohydrates first. Go for a simple dish such as grilled meat rather than a mixed au gratin dish. This will make it easier to adapt your choice to the food groups in your meal plan.
4)   Pay particular attention to amounts.
5)   Order food prepared with a minimum of fat, such as grilled skewered meats or poached fish.
6)   Do not eat chicken skin.

7) Ask for sauces and salad dressing on the side whenever possible.

8) Share your French fries, cake or pizza with a friend.

9) Order half-servings or servings from the children's menu.

10) Order two starters rather than a starter and a main course.

To learn how to estimate serving sizes at a glance, practice measuring and weighing food. Some people find that trial and error is the best way to learn to estimate the carbohydrate content of restaurant food. Serving sizes can also be estimated by comparing them to hand size. For more information, speak to a dietician.

Delayed Meals

1. How are blood glucose levels affected if a meal is delayed?

A delayed meal can lead to hypoglycemia if the person with diabetes injects insulin or takes medications that stimulate the pancreas to produce more insulin (for example, glyburide, gliclazide, repaglinide).

1) **If the meal is delayed by approximately one hour:**
   Have a snack providing 15 g of carbohydrates at the scheduled mealtime and subtract this amount from the usual carbohydrate content of the meal.

2) **If the meal is delayed two to three hours:**
   Have the equivalent of one or two servings of starches (15 g to 30 g of carbohydrates) with a small amount of protein. Then subtract these servings from the eventual meal or, if it is the evening meal, switch the evening snack with the delayed meal.

In all of these cases, take oral antidiabetic medications or insulin with the delayed meal.

Alcohol

1. **Can people with diabetes drink alcohol?**

   People with diabetes can drink alcohol if their diabetes is well controlled. It should always be remembered, however, that excessive alcohol consumption can affect blood glucose levels and can lead to increases in:
   1) blood pressure;
   2) triglycerides;
   3) weight.

2. **What effect does alcohol have on blood glucose?**

   There are two types of alcoholic drinks:
   1) **alcoholic drinks containing sugar;** these include beer, aperitif wines, and sweet wines. They can raise blood glucose;
   2) **alcoholic drinks that do not contain sugar;** these include dry wines and distilled alcohol such as gin, rye, rum, whisky, vodka, cognac, armagnac, and so on. They do not raise blood glucose if they are consumed in small quantities.

   Drinking alcohol on an empty stomach can cause hypoglycemia in people with diabetes, particularly those who inject insulin or take medications to stimulate the pancreas to produce insulin (for example, glyburide, gliclazide, repaglinide).

   All types of alcohol can trigger **late hypoglycemia**. If alcohol is consumed with the evening meal, it can produce nocturnal hypoglycemia.

   To avoid this risk:
   1) have a snack before bed;
   2) check blood glucose during the night, if recommended.

3. **What factors should be considered when drinking alcohol?**
   1) Alcohol has a **high calorie content**. Regular consumption can hinder weight loss or even cause weight gain, because the calories in the alcohol are added to the calories in the meal plan.
   2) Alcohol **does not belong to a food group in your meal plan.** Excessive drinking can

be harmful to your health, especially if highly nutritive foods are left out of the regular food plan.

3) Excessive drinking can increase **levels of triglycerides** (a type of blood fat) and **blood pressure**.

4. What are the main recommendations regarding alcohol consumption?

1) Drink alcohol only if your diabetes is well controlled.
2) Drink alcohol with food, never on an empty stomach.
3) Drink in moderation:
    o women should have no more than one drink a day (a maximum of nine a week);
    o men should have no more than two drinks a day (a maximum of fourteen a week).
4) Drink slowly.
5) Avoid drinking alcohol before, during or after physical activity.

> **One drink corresponds to:**
> 1 ½ oz (45 mL) of distilled alcohol
> 5 oz (150 mL) of dry red or white wine
> 2 oz (60 mL) of dry sherry
> 12 oz (340 mL) of beer

Remember:
  o Just one drink can cause hypoglycemia.
  o Just one drink is enough to make your breath smell like alcohol.
  o Because the symptoms of hypoglycemia and drunkenness are very similar, people around you may confuse the two and delay appropriate treatment. Wear a bracelet or pendant that identifies you as diabetic.

5. What are the calorie and carbohydrate contents of alcoholic drinks?

The following chart presents the calorie and carbohydrate contents of some alcoholic drinks.

Alcoholic drinks	Amount	Energy (calories)	Carbohydrates (grams)
Regular beer	340 mL (12 oz)	150	13
Light beer	340 mL (12 oz)	95	4
Beer with 0,5 % alcohol	340 mL (12 oz)	60 to 85	12 to 18
Low-carbohydrate beer	340 mL (12 oz)	90	2.5
Wine coolers	340 mL (12 oz)	170	22
Vodka Ice®, Tornade®	340 mL (12 oz)	260	50
Sweet sherry	60 mL (2 oz)	79	4
Sweet vermouth	60 mL (2 oz)	96	10
Scotch	45 mL (1½ oz)	98	0
Rhum	45 mL (1½ oz)	98	0
Dry white wine	150 mL (5 oz)	106	1
Dry red wine	150 mL (5 oz)	106	2
Champagne	150 mL (5 oz)	120	2.5
Porto	60 mL (2 oz)	91	7
Crème de menthe	45 mL (1½ oz)	143	21
Coffee liqueur	45 mL (1½ oz)	159	17
Cognac	45 mL (1½ oz)	112	0

6. What are some alternatives to alcoholic drinks?

Alcoholic drinks can be replaced with the following:

- low-sodium carbonated water;
- diet soft drinks;
- tomato juice with lemon or Tabasco sauce;
- water with lemon and ice.

Minor Illnesses

1. What effects do minor illnesses have on diabetes?

Minor illnesses such as a cold, the flu or gastroenteritis are sources of stress on the body and can destabilize and increase blood sugar levels. This occurs for two reasons:

- o   An increase in the secretion of certain hormones causes glucose stored in the liver to enter the bloodstream;
- o   These same hormones increase resistance to insulin and prevent glucose from entering the cells.

These two reactions can lead to hyperglycemia.

2. What precautions should be taken in the case of a minor illness?

If a person with diabetes has a cold or the flu but is not ill enough to warrant a visit to the doctor, he or she should follow these five rules:

1) **Continue taking oral antidiabetic medications or insulin.**

   Insulin needs can increase during an illness. Doctors can provide a sliding scale based on blood glucose readings to adjust insulin dosage for patients on insulin injection treatment. The following is an example:

   Add one unit of rapid-acting insulin (Apidra®, Humalog® or NovoRapid®) or short-acting insulin (Humulin® R or Novolin® ge Toronto) for every mmol/L higher than 14 mmol/L before each meal and at bedtime, and during the night if required.

2) **Check blood glucose levels at least four times a day or every two hours if they are high.**

3) **Check for ketone bodies in urine or blood when blood glucose is higher than 14 mmol/L.**

4) **Drink a lot of water to avoid dehydration.**

5) **Consume the recommended amount of carbohydrates in easily digested foods.**

3. Should the same precautions be taken for gastroenteritis?

Gastroenteritis generally causes diarrhea and vomiting that can in some cases lead to dehydration and a loss of electrolytes (such as sodium and potassium) because sufferers are unable to eat or drink.

Important!!!
See your doctor or go to the emergency room if any of the following situations occur:
1)   your blood glucose is higher than 20 mmol/L;
2)   urine or blood tests show moderate or large levels of ketone bodies;
3)   you are vomiting and cannot retain liquids;
4)   you have a fever with a temperature higher than 38.5°C (101.3°F) for more than 48 hours.

A three-phase approach will avoid dehydration and reduce diarrhea and vomiting:

Phase 1: Liquid food for the first 24 hours
Consume only liquids. In particular, drink water, bouillon or consommé at any time. Every hour, drink liquids containing about 15 g of carbohydrates. If you have trouble tolerating large amounts, try drinking 15 mL or 1 tablespoon every 15 minutes instead.

Commercially available oral rehydrating solutions such as Gastrolyte® and Pedialyte® are helpful, or try a homemade preparation: mix 250 mL (1 cup) of orange juice, the same amount of water, and 2 mL (½ tsp) of salt. One cup (250 mL) provides 15 g of carbohydrates.

Gradually replace these drinks with juice, flavoured gelatine, regular non-caffeinated flat soft drinks and nutritional supplements (such as Glucerna®, Resource Diabetic® or Boost Diabetic®, for example).

Phase 2: Low-residue foods (gentle on the large intestine)
Add solid foods gradually, increasing consumption by portions of 15 g of carbohydrates, until you reach the recommended carbohydrate content of the meal plan. For example:
- fruits: 1 small raw apple (grated), ½ a ripe banana, 125 mL (½ cup) unsweetened orange juice, etc.;
- starches: 2 rusks, 8 soda crackers, 4 melba toasts, 1 slice of toast, 75 mL (⅓ cup) of plain pasta or rice, etc.;
- vegetables: carrots, beets, asparagus, string or wax beans, etc.;
- meats: lean meats such as white chicken or turkey, fish cooked without fat, mild cheese, etc.

Phase 3: Eat normally

Gradually resume your normal diet according to the meal plan, but continue to limit your intake of certain items:

- foods that produce intestinal gas such as corn, legumes (chickpeas, red beans, and so on), cabbage, onions, garlic and raw vegetables;
- foods that are irritants, including anything fried or spiced, as well as chocolate, coffee, and cola.

Planning a Trip

1. How should a person with diabetes plan a trip?

When preparing for a trip, people with diabetes should take the following precautions.

1) Make sure your diabetes is **well controlled**.
2) Get a **doctor's letter** stating that you have diabetes and describing your treatment, particularly if you require insulin injections.
3) Carry a **piece of identification** or bracelet indicating that you have diabetes.
4) Find out what coverage is provided by **insurance companies** for pre-existing diseases incurring medical expenses abroad. Also find out whether your travel costs to get home in case of medical emergency are covered.
5) Find out about the **habits and customs** of the country you are visiting.
6) **Alert the transportation company** that you have diabetes.
7) Find out about the required vaccines or other treatments (for example, malaria prevention) from a **travellers' clinic** or your doctor.
8) Prepare a **medication kit** with treatments for diarrhea, vomiting and travel sickness. Include antibiotics if your doctor advises.
9) Bring at least two pairs of **comfortable shoes**.
10) **If possible, do not travel alone**.

2. Should any precautions be taken when travelling with equipment and medication for the treatment of diabetes?

Everything that is required to treat diabetes should be kept in a carry-on bag (not in stored luggage). The items should include the following:

1) All medications with the identifying pharmacy label.
2) Twice the normal amount of insulin required, in case some vials break or insulin is not available abroad. It should be noted that in some countries, insulin is packaged and sold in a different concentration (40 units/mL). When injecting, make sure the syringe corresponds to the concentration of insulin used.
3) An insulation kit to protect insulin.
4) Extra syringes, even if you use a pen-injector.
5) A self-monitoring kit (meter, test strips, etc.).
6) Emergency food provisions in case of hypoglycemia or a delayed meal (for example, dried or fresh fruits, juice, nuts, packets of peanut butter or cheese and crackers).

3. Is there any special advice for diabetic travellers?

When travelling, people with diabetes should heed the following recommendations:
1) Follow your regular meal and snack schedule as closely as possible.
2) Because your habits or routine could change, continue to check your blood glucose levels regularly to make sure the diabetes is still well controlled.
3) Always carry food provisions in case of hypoglycemia or a delayed meal (for example, dried or fresh fruits, juice, nuts, packets of peanut butter or cheese and crackers).
4) Check your feet daily to check for cuts or contusions;

4. How should people following the "split-mixed" insulin regimen adapt their insulin doses for time differences of more than three hours?

The "split-mixed" insulin regimen is a combination of intermediate-acting (Humulin® N or Novolin® ge NPH) and rapid-acting (Apidra®, Humalog® or NovoRapid ®) or short-acting insulin (Humulin® R or Novolin® ge Toronto), injected before the morning and evening meals.

Take for example a trip from Montreal to Paris with a six-hour time difference. Suppose you normally take the following insulin doses:
  o Novolin® ge NPH 16 units and NovoRapid® (NR) 8 units before breakfast;
  o Novolin® ge NPH 6 units and NovoRapid® (NR) 6 units before dinner.

Montreal to Paris:

The departure day will be six hours shorter, so **reduce the NPH dose by 50% before dinner. Eat only half of your dinner before leaving and the other half during the flight. Take 50% of the NR dose before dinner in Montreal and 50% before the evening in-flight meal.**

Meals	Blood glucose	Insulin	Meals
Montreal: breakfast	Yes	NPH 16 units NR 8 units	normal
Montreal: lunch	Yes	–	normal
Montreal: dinner	Yes	NPH 3 units NR 3 units	50%
In-flight: evening meal	Yes	NR 3 units	50%
In-flight: breakfast	Yes	NPH 16 units NR 8 units	normal

Paris-Montreal.

The return day will be six hours longer, so **have the evening meal during the flight** with the regular amount of NR insulin. Also, **have an additional evening meal** containing 50% of a regular evening meal's carbohydrates, **preceded by a dose of NR equal to 50% of the usual pre-dinner dose.** The NPH dose should be delayed until the second evening meal.

Meals	Blood glucose	Insulin	Meals
Paris: breakfast	Yes	NPH 16 units NR 8 units	normal
Paris: lunch	Yes	–	normal
In-flight: dinner	Yes	NR 6 units	normal
Montreal: evening meal	Yes	NPH 6 units NR 3 units	50%

5. How should people following the "multiple daily injections (MDI)" insulin regimen with fixed carbohydrates adapt their insulin doses for time differences of more than three hours?

The "MDI" insulin regimen with fixed carbohydrates consists of one injection of rapid-acting (Apidra®, Humalog® or NovoRapid®) or short-acting (Humulin® R or Novolin® ge Toronto) insulin before each meal and one injection of intermediate acting (Humulin® N or Novolin® ge NPH) or long-acting (Levemir® or Lantus®) insulin at bedtime.

The time difference between Montreal and Paris is six hours. Suppose you normally take:

- o   NovoRapid® (NR) 8 units before breakfast;
- o   NovoRapid® (NR) 8 units before lunch;
- o   NovoRapid® (NR) 8 units before dinner;
- o   Novolin® ge NPH 8 units before bedtime.

Montreal-Paris.
The departure day will be six hours shorter, so **move the NPH dose up before the dinner and take only 50% of it.** Have half the dinner meal before leaving and the other half during the in-flight evening meal. **Take 50% of the NR dose before dinner in Montreal and 50% before the in-flight evening meal.**

Meals	Blood glucose	Insulin	Meals
Montreal: breakfast	Yes	NR 8 units	normal
Montreal: lunch	Yes	NR 8 units	normal
Montreal: dinner	Yes	NPH 4 units NR 4 units	50%
In-flight: evening meal	Yes	NR 4 units	50%
In-flight: breakfast	Yes	NR 8 units	normal

Paris-Montreal:
The return day will be six hours longer, so eat the in-flight dinner with the regular amount of NR insulin. You should also eat **an additional evening meal** containing 50% of the usual evening meal carbohydrates, **preceded by 50% of the usual pre-dinner NR dose.** In addition, delay the NPH dose until bedtime.

Meals	Blood glucose	Insulin	Meals
Paris: breakfast	Yes	NR 8 units	normal
Paris: lunch	Yes	NR 8 units	normal
In-flight: dinner	Yes	NR 8 units	normal
Montreal: evening meal	Yes	NR 4 units	50%
Montreal: bedtime snack	Yes	NPH 8 units	snack

6. **How should people following the "multiple daily injection (MDI)" insulin regimen with variable carbohydrate adapt their insulin doses for time differences of more than three hours?**

The "MDI" insulin regimen with variable carbohydrates consists of one injection of rapid-acting (Apidra®, Humalog® or NovoRapid®) or short-acting (Humulin® R or Novolin® ge Toronto) insulin before each meal and one injection of intermediate acting (Humulin® N or Novolin® ge NPH) or long acting (Levemir® or Lantus®) insulin at bedtime.

The time difference between Montreal and Paris is six hours. Suppose you normally take:

- ○ Humalog® (Hg) 1.2 units/10 g of carbohydrates before breakfast;
- ○ Humalog® (Hg) 1.0 unit/10 g of carbohydrates before lunch;
- ○ Humalog® (Hg) 1.0 unit/10 g of carbohydrates before the evening meal;
- ○ Lantus® 12 units at bedtime.

Because long acting insulin (Lantus®) has an extended duration, it is not necessary to change the dose.

Montreal-Paris.

The departure day will be six hours shorter, so **move the Lantus® dose up before departure.** Although it is possible for people on the "MDI" insulin regimen with variable carbohydrates to wait and eat dinner on the plane, a **light meal before departure is recommended,** along with Hg insulin according to the amount of carbohydrates consumed. An in-flight evening meal is also possible, again with Hg insulin according to the amount of carbohydrates consumed. **The next morning during the flight, Hg insulin should be taken before breakfast as usual.**

Meals	Blood glucose	Insulin	Meals
Montreal: breakfast	Yes	Hg 1.2 units /10 g of carbohydrates	normal
Montreal: lunch	Yes	Hg 1.0 unit /10 g of carbohydrates	normal
Montreal: dinner	Yes	Lantus® 12 units; Hg 1.0 unit /10 g of carbohydrates	50%
In-flight: evening meal	Yes	Hg 1.0 unit /10 g of carbohydrates	normal or 50%
In-flight: breakfast	Yes	Hg 1.2 units /10 g of carbohydrates	normal

Paris-Montreal.
The return day will be six hours longer, so **eat the dinner during the flight with the same dose of Hg insulin, and eat an additional evening meal,** along with the usual pre-dinner dose of Hg. **Take Lantus® at bedtime as usual.**

Meals	Blood glucose	Insulin	Meals
Paris: breakfast	Yes	Hg 1.2 units /10 g of carbohydrates	normal
Paris: lunch	Yes	Hg 1.0 unit /10 g of carbohydrates	normal
In-flight: dinner	Yes	Hg 1.0 unit /10 g of carbohydrates	normal
Montreal: evening meal	Yes	Hg 1.0 unit /10 g of carbohydrates	normal or 50%
Montreal: bedtime snack	Yes	Lantus® 12 units	snack

7. **How should people following the "premixed" insulin regimen adapt their insulin doses for time differences of more than three hours?**

The "premixed" insulin regimen consists of one injection of a mix of rapid-acting or short-acting insulin and intermediate acting insulin (Humulin® 30/70, Novolin® ge 30/70, 50/50, 40/60, Humalog® Mix 25, etc.) before breakfast and dinner.

The time difference between Montreal and Paris is six hours. Suppose you normally take the following doses of Humulin® (H) 30/70:

- 20 units before breakfast;
- 10 units before dinner.

Montreal-Paris.

The departure day will be six hours shorter, so **have half the dinner meal before leaving and the other half during the in-flight evening meal.** Also, take **half the insulin dose for the dinner meal before leaving and the other half before the in-flight evening meal.**

Meals	Blood glucose	Insulin	Meals
Montreal: breakfast	Yes	H 30/70 20 units	normal
Montreal: lunch	Yes	–	normal
Montreal: dinner	Yes	H 30/70 5 units	50%
In-flight: evening meal	Yes	H 30/70 5 units	50%
In-flight: breakfast	Yes	H 30/70 20 units	normal

Paris-Montreal.

The return day will be six hours longer, so **have an additional evening meal** (50% of the usual carbohydrate content) **preceded by a dose of insulin equivalent to 50% of the usual pre-dinner dose.**

Meals	Blood glucose	Insulin	Meals
Paris: breakfast	Yes	H 30/70 20 units	normal
Paris: lunch	Yes	---	normal
In-flight: dinner	Yes	H 30/70 10 units	normal
Montreal: evening meal	Yes	H 30/70 5 units	50%
Montreal: bedtime snack	Yes	–	snack

Oral Antidiabetic Drugs

1. **What are oral antidiabetic drugs?**

   Oral antidiabetic drugs are medications taken **orally to lower blood glucose levels.**

2. **When should oral antidiabetic drugs be used to treat diabetes?**

   Oral antidiabetic drugs are used to treat type 2 diabetes **if diet, exercise and weight loss programs are not sufficient to normalize blood glucose levels.** They can be taken alone or in combination.

   WARNING! Oral antidiabetic drugs are complementary treatments. They **do not replace** diet, exercise and weight loss programs.

3. How many classes of oral antidiabetic drugs are there?

There are seven classes of oral antidiabetic drugs:

Class	Drug
Sulfonylureas*	Chlorpropamide (e.g., Apo®- Chlorpropamide) Gliclazide (e.g., Diamicron®) Glimepiride (Amaryl®) Glyburide (e.g., Diaβeta®, Euglucon®) Tolbutamide (e.g., Apo®-Tolbutamide)
Amino acid derivatives* Meglitinides*	Nateglinide (Starlix®) Repaglinide (GlucoNorm®)
Biguanides	Metformin (e.g., Glucophage®)
Thiazolidinediones	Pioglitazone (Actos®) Rosiglitazone (Avandia®)
Alpha-glucosidase inhibitors	Acarbose (Glucobay®)
Dipeptidyl peptidase-4 (DPP-4) inhibitors	Sitagliptin (Januvia®)

* Insulin secretagogues

4. What are the characteristics of sulfonylureas (e.g., Diaβeta®, Diamicron®, Amaryl®)?

1) **Mechanism of action:** Sulfonylureas **stimulate the pancreas to produce more insulin** (they are known as insulin secretagogues). They are therefore ineffective if the insulin-producing cells of the pancreas no longer function.

2) **Adverse effects: Hypoglycemia** is the adverse effect most commonly attributed to sulfonylureas. It can occur at any time of day or night; dosage should therefore be adjusted accordingly. To minimize the risk of hypoglycemia, meals and snacks should be eaten on a regular schedule as set out in the meal plan. Sulfonylureas should not be taken at bedtime.

3) **When to take them:** Sulfonylureas should be taken **before meals, but never more than 30 minutes beforehand.** Sulfonylureas that are taken once a day, such as modified release gliclazide (Diamicron® MR) and glimepiride (Amaryl®), should be taken with breakfast.

5. **What are the characteristics of nateglinide (Starlix®) and repaglinide (GlucoNorm®)?**

   1) **Mechanism of action:** Like sulfonylureas, nateglinide and repaglinide **stimulate the pancreas to produce more insulin** (they are insulin secretagogues). They are therefore ineffective if the insulin-producing cells of the pancreas no longer function. They are faster and shorter acting than sulfonylureas.

   2) **Adverse effects: Hypoglycemia** is the adverse effect most commonly attributed to nateglinide and repaglinide. Dosage should be adjusted accordingly. To minimize the risk of hypoglycemia, meals and snacks should be eaten according to a regular schedule as set out in the meal plan. Nateglinide and repaglinide should not be taken at bedtime.

   3) **When to take them:** They should be taken as close as possible to the beginning of a meal (0 to 15 minutes), but never more than 30 minutes beforehand.

6. **What are the characteristics of metformin (for example, Glucophage®)?**

   1) **Mechanism of action:** The primary action of metformin is to **reduce the production of glucose by the liver.** It also lowers insulin resistance or, in other words, renders insulin more efficient.

   2) **Adverse effects: Intestinal problems**, especially diarrhea, are the side effects most commonly attributed to metformin. Some patients also note a slight metallic aftertaste. When taken on its own, metformin is very rarely associated with hypoglycemia.

   3) **When to take it:** Take metformin at mealtime in order to minimize adverse intestinal effects.

7. **What are the characteristics of pioglitazone (Actos®) and rosiglitazone (Avandia®)?**

   1) **Mechanism of action:** Pioglitazone and rosiglitazone **lower insulin resistance** or, in other words, increase the effectiveness of insulin. This results in an increase in the use of glucose by muscle tissue in particular and by adipose (fatty) tissue.

   2) **Adverse effects: Edema (swelling due to water retention) and weight gain** are possible adverse effects. These drugs must be used with caution or avoided by

people with cardiovascular disease. When taken on their own, pioglitazone and rosiglitazone are generally not associated with hypoglycemia.

3) **When to take them:** These drugs should always be taken at the same time of day, usually in the morning. They do not have to be taken with meals.

8. What are the characteristics of acarbose (Glucobay®)?

1) **Mechanism of action:** Acarbose **slows the absorption of carbohydrates ingested at meals.** It also helps control rising blood glucose levels **after meals.**

2) **Adverse effects:** The adverse effects most commonly attributed to acarbose are **intestinal problems, particularly bloating and flatulence (gas).** When taken on its own, acarbose is not associated with hypoglycemia.

3) **When to take it:** To ensure effectiveness, acarbose should be taken with the first mouthful of a meal.

9. What are the characteristics of sitagliptin (Januvia®)?

1) **Mechanism of action:** Sitagliptin **intensifies the effect of certain intestinal hormones** (such as GLP-1) involved in the control of blood sugar. It causes an increase in insulin secretion and decrease in the secretion of glucagon (a hyperglycemic hormone), but only if blood sugar is high.

2) **Adverse effects:** DPP-4 inhibitors such as sitagliptin are generally well tolerated. When taken alone, sitagliptin is very rarely associated with hypoglycemia.

3) **When to take it:** This drug should always be taken at the same time of the day, usually in the morning. It is not necessary to take it with food.

10. What should be done if a dose is missed?

1) If you notice the omission quickly, take the dose immediately. If not, skip the missed dose and wait for the next scheduled one.

2) **Never double the dose.**

3) It is not a good idea to take sulfonylureas, nateglinide or repaglinide at bedtime, as they can cause a risk of nocturnal hypoglycemia.

4) Acarbose is effective only if it is taken **with a meal.** If forgotten at mealtime, there is no point in taking it afterwards.

11. Why are antidiabetic drugs taken together?

Any given class of antidiabetic drugs acts according to a particular mechanism. Secretagogues, for example, stimulate the release of insulin via the pancreas, while biguanides decrease the production of glucose by the liver. In many cases, combining agents with different modes of action is a way to increase the effectiveness of treatment.

12. Do oral antidiabetic drugs interact with other medications?

All drugs can potentially interact with other agents. The responsibility for anticipating and preventing such interactions falls on pharmacists and doctors, but the patient also has a role to play.

People taking medication should keep an up-to-date list of their prescriptions, ideally one provided by their pharmacist. They are strongly advised to **bring their medication containers** when seeing the doctor, who will use them to guide any decisions about treatment. It is also a good idea for people with diabetes to use the same pharmacist at all times; in such a case, the pharmacist will be better able to detect potential problems and advise appropriately (regarding duplicate prescriptions, adverse effects or interactions, for example).

13. Are oral antidiabetic drugs lifelong treatments?

At this point, diabetes is a disease that can be controlled but not cured. Generally speaking, therefore, oral antidiabetic drugs are long-term treatments. The doctor will regularly adjust treatment, either increasing or decreasing dosages. The goal of such treatment is to **normalize** blood glucose levels without causing adverse effects such as hypoglycemia.

MOST COMMON ORAL ANTIDIABETIC DRUGS

Drug	Glyburide	Gliclazide	Modified release Gliclazide	Glimepiride
Class	Sulfonylureas (insulin secretagogues)	Sulfonylureas (insulin secretagogues)	Sulfonylureas (insulin secretagogues)	Sulfonylureas (insulin secretagogues)
Brand name (non-exhaustive list)	Diaβeta Euglucon Apo-Glyburide Gen-Glybe Novo-Glyburide	Diamicron Gen-Gliclazide Novo-Gliclazide	Diamicron MR	Amaryl
Form marketed	2.5 mg and 5 mg tablets (divisible into two)	80 mg tablets (divisible into four)	30 mg tablets (non-divisible)	1 mg, 2 mg and 4 mg tablets (divisible into two)
Daily dosage	1.25 mg to 20 mg	40 mg to 320 mg	30 mg to 120 mg	1 mg to 8 mg
Number of daily doses	1 to 3	1 to 3	1	1
When to take it	0 to 30 mins. before meals	0 to 30 mins. before meals	With breakfast	With breakfast
Most common adverse effects	Hypoglycemia	Hypoglycemia	Hypoglycemia	Hypoglycemia
Risk of hypoglycemia	Yes	Yes	Yes	Yes

Repaglinide	Nateglinide	Acarbose	Metformin	Extended release metformin	Sitagliptin
Meglitinides (insulin secretagogues)	Amino acid derivative (insulin secretagogue)	Alpha-glucosidase inhibitor	Biguanides	Biguanides	Dipeptidyl peptidase-4 inhibitor
GlucoNorm	Starlix	Glucobay	Glucophage Apo-Metformin Gen-Metformin Novo-Metformin	Glumetza	Januvia
0.5 mg, 1 mg and 2 mg tablets (non-divisible)	60 mg, 120 mg and 180 mg tablets (non-divisible)	50 mg and 100 mg tablets (divisible into two)	500 mg tablets (divisible into two) and 850 mg tablets (non-divisible)	500 mg and 1000 mg tablets	100 mg tablets (non-divisible)
1 mg to 16 mg	180 mg to 540 mg	50 mg to 300 mg	250 mg to 2500 mg	500 mg to 2000 mg	100 mg
2 to 4 (according to the number of meals)	3	1 to 3	1 to 4	1	1
0 to 15 mins. before meals	0 to 15 mins. before meals	With the first bite of a meal	With meals	With dinner	With or without food
Hypoglycemia	Hypoglycemia	Bloating, flatulence, diarrhea	Diarrhea/metallic taste	Diarrhea	Well tolerated
Yes	Yes	No	No	No	No

Drug	Rosiglitazone	Rosiglitazone and metformin	Rosiglitazone and glimepiride	Pioglitazone
Class	Thiazolidinediones	Thiazolidinediones and biguanides	Thiazolidinediones and sulfonylureas	Thiazolidinediones
Brand name (non-exhaustive list)	Avandia	Avandamet	Avandaryl	Actos
Form marketed	2 mg, 4 mg and 8 mg tablets (non-divisible)	1 mg/500 mg, 2 mg/500 mg 4 mg/500 mg 2 mg/1000 mg 4 mg/1000 mg tablets (rosiglitazone/metformine) (non-divisible)	4 mg/1 mg 4 mg/2 mg 4 mg/4 mg tablets (rosiglitazone/ glimepiride)	15 mg, 30 mg and 45 mg tablets (non-divisible)
Daily dosage	4 mg to 8 mg	2 mg/1000 mg to 8 mg/2000 mg	4 mg/1 mg to 4 mg/4 mg	15 mg to 45 mg
Number of daily doses	1 to 2	2	1	1
When to take it	With or without food	With meals	With breakfast	With or without food
Most common adverse effects	Edema/weight gain	Edema/weight gain/diarrhea/metallic taste	Edema, weight gain, hypoglycemia	Edema/weight gain
Risk of hypoglycemia	No	No	Yes	No

MECHANISM OF ACTION OF ORAL ANTIDIABETIC DRUGS

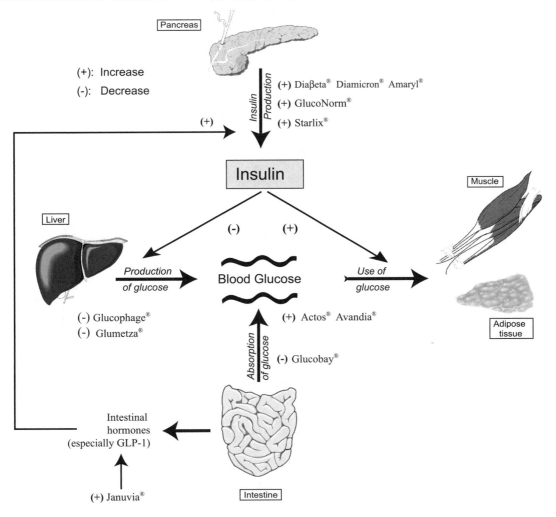

(+): Increase

(−): Decrease

(+) DiaβetaⓇ DiamicronⓇ AmarylⓇ

(+) GlucoNormⓇ

(+) StarlixⓇ

Insulin Production

(+)

Insulin

Liver

(−)   (+)

Muscle

Production of glucose

Blood Glucose

Use of glucose

(−) GlucophageⓇ
(−) GlumetzaⓇ

(+) ActosⓇ AvandiaⓇ

Adipose tissue

Absorption of glucose

(−) GlucobayⓇ

Intestinal hormones (especially GLP-1)

(+) JanuviaⓇ

Intestine

- o DiaβetaⓇ, DiamicronⓇ, AmarylⓇ, GlucoNormⓇ and StarlixⓇ stimulate the pancreas to produce more insulin (insulin secretagogues).
- o GlucophageⓇ (metformin) decreases the production of glucose by the liver.
- o ActosⓇ and AvandiaⓇ augments the action of insulin, which in turn increases the use of glucose by the muscle tissue in particular, and by adipose (fatty) tissue.
- o GlucobayⓇ delays the absorption of dietary carbohydrates.
- o JanuviaⓇ (sitagliptin) enhances the action of certain intestinal hormones (such as GLP-1) that increase the secretion of insulin by the pancreas when blood glucose is high.

Over-the-counter Drugs

1. What are over-the-counter drugs?

Over-the-counter drugs include all medications sold without prescription. Some may be obtained only after consulting a pharmacist, although most can be purchased on the spot.

2. When and how should over-the-counter drugs be used?

Over-the-counter drugs allow people to self-medicate for **mild health problems**. They should only be used for **short periods of time** to ensure that they are not masking the symptoms of a more serious condition. All directions and warnings printed on the product's packaging should be followed closely.

3. Are over-the-counter drugs free of side effects?

No drug is completely free of side effects. Certain over-the-counter drugs can cause adverse effects in some cases. Some drugs should be avoided or used with caution by people with certain illnesses. There is also a risk of interactions between over-the-counter and prescription drugs.

4. How can I be sure that the over-the-counter drugs I choose are safe?

It is strongly recommended that you speak with your pharmacist before selecting an over-the-counter drug. Your pharmacist can recommend the most suitable product for your condition, taking into account your symptoms, health problems, and any other drugs you are taking, possibly even suggesting non-pharmacological alternatives. The pharmacist will recommend that you see your doctor if he or she believes that your condition requires it. Always have your prescriptions filled by the same pharmacist; this will ensure that your file is always up-to-date and that the pharmacist has all the information necessary to properly advise you.

5. Which over-the-counter drugs should be avoided or used with caution by people with diabetes?

The following drugs should be used with caution:

1) oral decongestants (for the treatment of nasal congestion);
2) medications containing sugar;
3) keratolytic preparations (for the treatment of corns, calluses and warts);
4) high doses of acetylsalicylic acid or ASA (e.g., Aspirin®).

6. Why should oral decongestants be used with caution?

Oral decongestants (e.g., Sudafed®) are medications in syrup, tablet or powder form that reduce nasal congestion. Most oral decongestants contain what is known as a "sympathomimetic" ingredient (e.g., pseudoephedrine) that can have a **hyperglycemic** effect, especially if recommended doses are exceeded. These types of products are frequently overconsumed. Cold medications often contain a mixture of ingredients (to relieve coughs, fight fevers, etc.), including a sympathomimetic decongestant. It is not uncommon for people to take two different products when treating a cold or the flu, thereby unwittingly doubling the dosage of the decongestant.

This type of oral decongestant is also not recommended for people with vascular problems, high blood pressure, hyperthyroidism or cardiac diseases such as angina.

Recommended alternative treatments include drinking plenty of water, keeping the room humidified and using a saline nasal vaporizer. If the condition persists, a nasal decongestant vaporizer may be used, but for no longer than 72 hours (to avoid rebound congestion).

7. Why should drugs containing sugar be used cautiously?

People with diabetes need to know which drugs contain sugar so that they do not unwittingly hamper their control of their blood glucose levels. Sugar is found not only in syrups, but also in powders, chewable tablets, lozenges, etc. People with diabetes must avoid any drug that contains more than **20 calories** (5 g of carbohydrates) **per dose or provides more than 80 calories** (20 g of carbohydrates) **per day**. If these drugs are taken on occasion, they should be included in the overall carbohydrate tally of the meal plan. If the sugar content of a product is not printed on the packaging, the pharmacist can provide this information.

There are a number of "sucrose-free" or "sugar-free" preparations. They usually contain sugar substitutes and can be used by people with diabetes at the recommended dose, as long as the active ingredient is not contraindicated for another reason.

8. Why should keratolytic preparations (for the treatment of corns, calluses and warts) be used with caution?

Adhesive plasters, pads, ointments or gels containing products such as salicylic or tannic acid are often used to treat corns, calluses and warts. These acids are highly irritating. See a doctor, a podiatrist or a nurse specializing in foot care before using these products.

9. Why should high doses of acetylsalicylic acid be used with caution?

High doses of acetylsalicylic acid (e.g., Aspirin®, ASA, Anacin®, Entrophen®, etc.) can cause **hypoglycemia** if the daily dose exceeds 4,000 mg, the equivalent of more than 12 tablets of 325 mg per day or more than 8 tablets of 500 mg each.

Acetaminophen (e.g., Tylenol®, Atasol®, etc.) does not contain acetylsalicylic acid and is a safe alternative for the treatment of fever and pain.

10. Is there a simple way at the pharmacy to find out which over-the-counter drugs should be used with caution or avoided?

In Quebec, the Ordre des pharmaciens du Québec has developed a program called the "Code médicament" ("Drug Caution Code"). It consists of six letters, each letter corresponding to a specific warning. These code letters usually appear on the price sticker or the particular shelf where the medication is placed.

Code letter "E" specifically concerns people with diabetes. Products bearing an "**E**" are **not recommended**. There are three types:
1) oral decongestants;
2) drugs with a sugar content in the recommended dose that equals 20 calories or more **per dose** or 80 calories or more **per day**;
3) keratolytic preparations (for the treatment of corns, calluses and warts).

In Quebec, a personalized "code médicament" card from your pharmacist will indicate the code letters that apply to you.

Elsewhere, ask your pharmacist whether there is a similar program in your area.

11. Can "natural health products" be used by people with diabetes?

There are a number of so-called "natural health products" on the market; it is important, however, to know that "natural" does not necessarily mean "harmless". In fact, some natural health products can have adverse effects, interact with prescribed drugs or be contraindicated for various illnesses.

In addition, the quality of natural health products on the market can vary widely, and it is not always possible to know exactly what they contain. An eight-digit natural product number (NPN) identifies products that are authorized for sale in Canada.

People with diabetes who choose to use a natural health product should ask a pharmacist to confirm whether the product is suitable. Doctors should also be informed of the products their patients use.

12. Can natural health products affect blood glucose levels?

Some natural health products can raise blood glucose levels, while others can lower them. For example, glucosamine, a supplement used for osteoarthritis, can increase glucose levels. Animal studies have also shown that it increases insulin resistance, although the effect of glucosamine on humans appears to be minimal. Nevertheless, because data is limited, people who decide to take glucosamine are advised to measure blood glucose levels regularly to observe the effects. Products that can lower blood glucose include fenugrec, vanadium, bitter melon (Momordica charantia), Gymnema sylvestre, chromium, American ginseng, and ivy gourd (*Coccinia grandis*).

It is generally advisable to consult a pharmacist or doctor before taking a natural health product to make sure it is both safe and effective. People with diabetes who decide to take a potentially hyperglycemic or hypoglycemic product should take care to observe its effect on their blood glucose levels.

According to currently available information and research, there are no natural products that can be recommended to replace oral antidiabetic drugs or insulin.

Insulins

1. ## What is the role of insulin?
    Insulin is a hormone that plays an important role in controlling blood glucose. It acts as a kind of "manager", keeping blood glucose levels down by allowing the glucose in the blood to enter the cells of the body and lowering the production of glucose by the liver.

2. ## When is insulin an appropriate treatment for diabetes?
    Insulin is routinely used to treat **type 1 diabetes** because in this form of the disease, the pancreas does not produce insulin. It can also be used for **type 2 diabetes** if diet, exercise, weight loss and oral antidiabetic drugs are not enough to control blood glucose. Insulin is not necessarily a last resort treatment. Earlier use of insulin may be necessary to control high blood sugar levels.

3. ## How are insulins produced?
    Insulins are primarily manufactured in laboratories through biogenetic techniques using genetically programmed bacteria or yeast.

    There are two categories of insulin:
    1) **Human insulin:** This type is identical to the insulin produced by the pancreas. All insulins called Humulin® or Novolin® belong to this category.
    2) **Analogue insulin:** This type is similar to the insulin produced by the pancreas, although its structure has been slightly modified in order to give it new properties.

Some examples of this type include Apidra®, Humalog®, NovoRapid,® NovoMix,® Lantus® and Levemir®.

Some types of insulin are of animal origin (purified pork insulin), but they are rarely used. They are mentioned here for informational purposes only.

4. What are the different types of insulin?

Insulins are classified according to their action time:

- o **onset of action:** the time insulin takes to start working;
- o **peak of action:** the time during which the insulin is at maximum effectiveness;
- o **duration of action:** the duration of the insulin's effectiveness in the body.

There are six types of insulin:

1) rapid-acting;
2) short-acting;
3) intermediate-acting;
4) long-acting;
5) **premixed insulin** made of a mixture of rapid-acting and intermediate-acting insulins;
6) **premixed insulin** made of a mixture of short-acting and intermediate-acting insulins.

5. What are the action times of the different types of insulin?

Type of insulin	Onset of action	Peak of action	Duration of action
Rapid-acting			
Apidra® (glulisine) Humalog® (lispro) NovoRapid® (aspart)	0 to 15 minutes 0 to15 minutes 0 to 10 minutes	1 to 1,5 hour 1 to 2 hours 1 to 3 hours	3 to 4 hours 3 to 4 hours 3 to 5 hours
Short-acting			
Humulin® R (Regular) Novolin® ge Toronto	30 minutes	2 to 4 hours	6 to 8 hours
Intermediate-acting			
Humulin® N Novolin® ge NPH	1 to 2 hours	6 to 12 hours	18 to 24 hours
Long-acting			
Lantus® (glargine) Levemir® (detemir)	1 hour 1 to 3 hours	Insignificant Insignificant	24 hours 20 to 24 hours
Premixed rapid-acting and intermediate-acting			
Humalog® Mix 25* Humalog® Mix 50*	0 to 15 minutes	1 to 2 hours and 6 to 12 hours	18 to 24 hours
NovoMix® 30**	10 to 20 minutes	1 to 4 hours	up to 24 hours
Premixed short-acting and intermediate-acting*			
Humulin® 30/70 Novolin® ge 30/70 Novolin® ge 40/60 Novolin® ge 50/50	30 minutes	2 to 4 hours and 6 to 12 hours	18 to 24 hours

*   Humalog® Mix 25 is a mixture of 25% lispro insulin (rapid-acting insulin) and 75% lispro protamine insulin (intermediate-acting insulin).
Humalog® Mix 50 is a mixture of 50% each of these two types of insulin.

** NovoMix® 30 is a mixture of 30% aspart insulin (rapid-acting insulin) and 70% aspart protamine insulin (intermediate-acting insulin)

***The first number corresponds to the percentage of short-acting insulin and the second to the percentage of intermediate-acting NPH insulin.
Note: The values indicated in the table may vary from one individual to another.

TIME-ACTION PROFILE OF THE DIFFERENT TYPES OF INSULIN

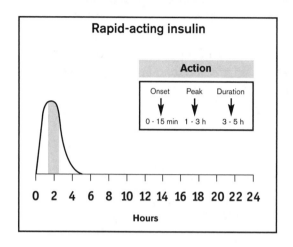

Rapid-acting insulin

Action		
Onset	Peak	Duration
↓	↓	↓
0 - 15 min	1 - 3 h	3 - 5 h

Hours

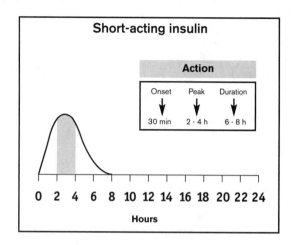

Short-acting insulin

Action		
Onset	Peak	Duration
↓	↓	↓
30 min	2 - 4 h	6 - 8 h

Hours

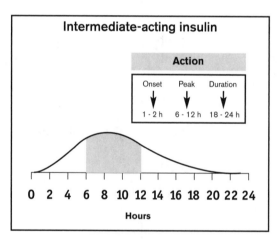

Intermediate-acting insulin

Action		
Onset	Peak	Duration
↓	↓	↓
1 - 2 h	6 - 12 h	18 - 24 h

Hours

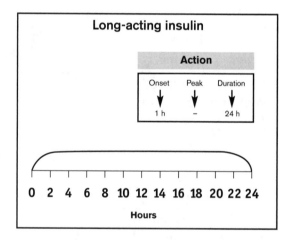

Long-acting insulin

Action		
Onset	Peak	Duration
↓	↓	↓
1 h	–	24 h

Hours

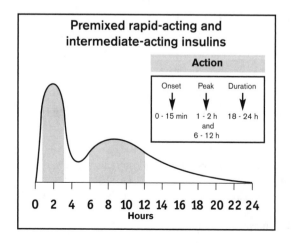

Premixed rapid-acting and intermediate-acting insulins

Action		
Onset	Peak	Duration
↓	↓	↓
0 - 15 min	1 - 2 h and 6 - 12 h	18 - 24 h

Hours

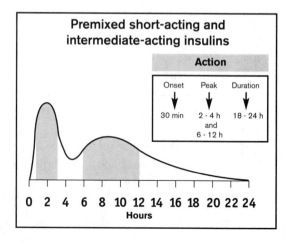

Premixed short-acting and intermediate-acting insulins

Action		
Onset	Peak	Duration
↓	↓	↓
30 min	2 - 4 h and 6 - 12 h	18 - 24 h

Hours

6. How many insulin injections are required daily?

In general, insulin therapy requires from one to four injections daily. The number and timing of injections as well as the types of insulin vary from one person to another, and treatment is adapted to his or her lifestyle. The goal is to maintain blood glucose levels as close as possible to normal.

7. What are the most frequently prescribed insulin regimens?

There are several insulin regimens. Here are four of the most frequently prescribed:

1) The "**split-mixed**" regimen consists of injecting intermediate-acting and rapid or short-acting insulin before breakfast and dinner. The injection of intermediate-acting insulin before the evening meal is sometimes administered at bedtime to control glucose levels overnight and to help prevent nocturnal hypoglycemia.

2) The "**basal-prandial**" regimen consists of injecting rapid-acting or short-acting insulin before each meal and intermediate-acting or long-acting basal insulin at bedtime (also called and MDI regimen i.e. multiple daily injections). Although basal insulin is usually administered in one injection, it can also be given as two (occasionally more) injections throughout the day.

   The rapid-acting or short-acting insulin dose may be fixed (fixed carbohydrate diet) or may correspond to the amount of carbohydrates consumed in the meal (variable carbohydrate diet). In a variable carbohydrate diet, the dose is defined as a ratio, as in 1 unit: 10 g of carbohydrates (1 unit of insulin for every 10 g of carbohydrates consumed).

3) The "**premixed**" regimen involves injecting a mixed dose of rapid-acting or short-acting insulin and intermediate-acting insulin before breakfast and dinner.

4) The "**combined**" regimen involves injecting intermediate-acting or long-acting insulin in combination with antidiabetic oral medication taken during the day.

8. What is intensive insulin therapy?

Intensive insulin therapy consists of multiple insulin injections (for example, the "basal-prandial" regimen) or the use of an insulin pump, combined with monitoring blood glucose measurements and self-adjusted insulin doses. This therapy tries to imitate the normal release of insulin from the pancreas. The goal is to maintain blood glucose levels as close as possible to normal.

9. How much insulin is required to control blood glucose?

Insulin doses are initially determined by the doctor and vary according to blood glucose readings. The doses are measured in **units**. Some people inject fixed doses and others calculate their doses according to the carbohydrate content of meals. Whatever the regimen, doses should be regularly modified according to factors such as diet, exercise and illness.

10. How should insulin injections be timed in relation to meals and bedtime?

Meals:

- o **Rapid-acting insulin** should be injected **just before meals** (or in the case of Apidra® and Humalog®, no more than 15 minutes before and NovoRapid®, no more than 10 minutes before), whether or not the insulin is premixed. Sometimes, rapid-acting insulin can be injected immediately after a meal, for example, when the carbohydrate intake cannot be estimated at the beginning of the meal.

- o **Short-acting insulin** should be injected **15 to 30 minutes before** meals, whether or not it is premixed.

   This allows the peak action of the insulin to coincide with the peak absorption of the carbohydrates consumed.

Bedtime:

- o **Intermediate-acting or long-acting insulin** is generally injected at approximately **10 p.m.** The injection time should be as regular as possible.

   In the case of intermediate-acting insulin, the peak action coincides with breakfast.

OPTIMAL INSULIN INJECTION TIMES

Insulin	Optimal Injection Time
Apidra® Humalog® NovoRapid® Humalog® Mix NovoMix®	• Immediately before meals (at the most, 10 minutes beforehand for Novo and 15 minutes beforehand for Apidra and Humalog). • May be administered immediately after meals (e.g., in the case of variable appetite and unpredictable dietary intake).
Humulin® R Novolin® ge Toronto Humulin® 30/70 Novolin® ge 30/70, 40/60, 50/50	• 15 to 30 minutes before meals.
Humulin® N Novolin® ge NPH	• If taken at bedtime, always at the same time, usually around 10 p.m. • If at breakfast and supper, at the same time as rapid or short-acting insulin
Lantus® Levemir®	• Always at the same time, usually at bedtime, around 10 p.m. • If twice a day, in the morning and at bedtime or with supper

11. What is the most common adverse effect of insulin treatment?

Hypoglycemia is the most common adverse effect seen in people taking insulin. The risk of hypoglycemia is much higher when insulin action is at its peak. Being well-informed about insulin and the rules governing dosage adjustment can lower the risk.

12. How can insulin be used to effectively control diabetes?

To control diabetes with insulin injections, it is important to:

1) closely follow your **meal plan;**
2) **check blood glucose levels regularly;**
3) **be well-informed about the insulin you use;** and
4) **self-adjust** your insulin doses after receiving the necessary training from your diabetes health care team.

13. What time of day should a person with diabetes who is taking insulin check blood glucose?

A person with diabetes on insulin treatment should measure blood glucose before meals and at bedtime (before a snack). It is also helpful to occasionally measure blood glucose after meals (two hours after the first mouthful) or during the night (around 2 a.m.) to check for nocturnal hypoglycemia. If the person is sick, blood glucose measurements should be taken more often. It should also be measured every time the person feels discomfort that could indicate hypoglycemia or hyperglycemia.

MAIN INSULIN REGIMENS

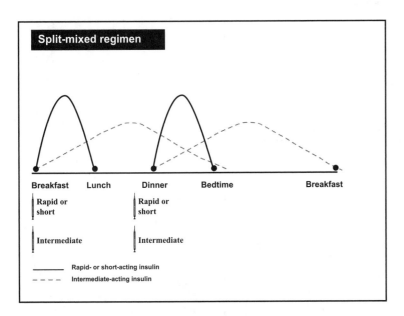

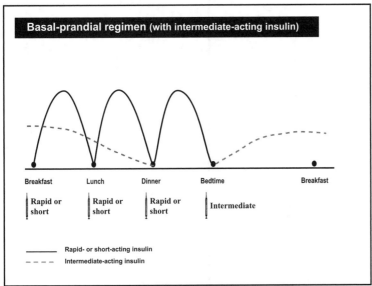

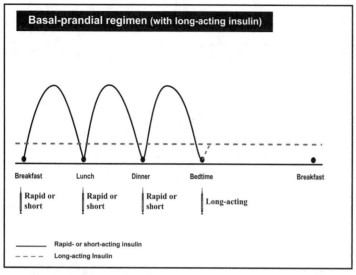

Basal-prandial regimen (with long-acting insulin)

| Breakfast | Lunch | Dinner | Bedtime | Breakfast |

Rapid or short | Rapid or short | Rapid or short | Long-acting

——— Rapid- or short-acting insulin
– – – Long-acting Insulin

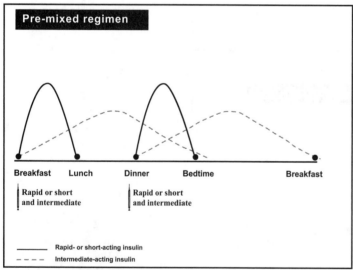

Pre-mixed regimen

| Breakfast | Lunch | Dinner | Bedtime | Breakfast |

Rapid or short and intermediate | Rapid or short and intermediate

——— Rapid- or short-acting insulin
– – – Intermediate-acting insulin

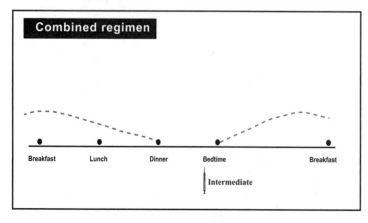

Combined regimen

| Breakfast | Lunch | Dinner | Bedtime | Breakfast |

Intermediate

Preparation and Injection of Insulin

1. What devices are used to inject insulin?

Two types of devices are available for insulin injection

1) **The syringe**: This device consists of a cylinder and a plunger equipped with a fine needle. Syringes have different capacities: 100 units, 50 units or 30 units. The finer the needle, the greater the gauge (for instance, a 30-gauge needle is finer than a 29-gauge needle). In addition, the finer the needle, the shorter it is (8 mm as opposed to 12.7 mm). Syringes also come with different scale graduations (½ unit, 1 unit and 2 units).

2) **The pen-injector**: This device is slightly larger than a pen and consists of three parts: the cap, which covers the pen, the cartridge-holder, which contains the insulin cartridge, and the pen body, which contains the plunger. A dosage ring allows you to select the desired dose.

2. What is involved in preparing and injecting a specific type of insulin with a syringe?

There are three steps involved in preparing and injecting a specific type of insulin with a syringe.

Preparing the materials

1) **Wash your hands** with soap and water and dry them well.
2) Lay out the **materials**: syringe, insulin vial, alcohol swab, cotton ball.
   - Use a new syringe for each injection.
   - Use a vial of insulin stored at room temperature.

3) Check the label of the vial to make sure you have the right **type of insulin**.

4) Check the **expiry dates** on the label: the date printed by the manufacturer and the date recorded after the vial was opened (*see the table in chapter 17 on pages 154-155 listing the temperatures and maximum storage times recommended by insulin manufacturers*).

   o **Do not prepare syringes in advance if the insulin used is Lantus®
   (glargine), which becomes foggy, or Levemir® (detemir), or Apidra
   (glulisine), because of a lack of information regarding its stability.**

Drawing up the insulin

1) If the **contents are opaque**, roll the vial between your hands and turn it upside down to mix the suspension well (**do not shake**). Replace the vial and place it on the table.

2) Disinfect the cap of the vial with the alcohol swab.

3) **Pull back the plunger** of the syringe to draw up an amount of air equal to the amount of insulin to be injected.

4) **Insert the needle** in the rubber cap of the insulin vial.

5) **Inject the air** into the vial.

6) **Turn the vial and syringe** upside down.

7) **Pull the plunger back slowly** to draw up the number of insulin units to be injected.

   o Make sure there are no air bubbles in the syringe; bubbles may cause a smaller amount of insulin to be injected.

   o Push and pull the plunger until any air bubbles disappear.

   o Check the syringe to make sure no insulin has been lost; if there has, repeat this step.

Injecting the insulin and recording the data

1) **Choose the injection area.**

   o Avoid injecting insulin into a limb or part of the body used for any physical activity (for example, a thigh if you intend to take a walk, an arm if you intend to play tennis, etc.).

2) **Choose the injection site** in the area, paying attention to the condition of the skin.

   o Avoid any crease, bump, growth, bruise, blotch or painful spot.

3) **Wash the skin** with soapy water, rinse and let dry.

   o Make sure the injection site is clean. The use of alcohol at home is optional.

4) **Pinch the skin between the thumb and forefinger and keep it pinched** until the end of the injection.

5) Hold the syringe like a pencil and **pierce the skin**.
   - o The insulin should be injected into subcutaneous tissue (tissue beneath the skin).
6) **Inject all the insulin**, pushing the plunger all the way.
   - o **Do not pull the plunger back:** raising the plunger to check whether the injection is at the right spot can damage the skin.
   - o **Leave the needle in place** for about **5 seconds**.
7) **Withdraw the needle** and carefully press the cotton ball to the injection site.
8) **Record the number of insulin units** injected as well as the type of insulin in the appropriate column of the self-monitoring logbook.

3.   What precautions should be taken when mixing two types of insulin in the same syringe?

When mixing clear and opaque insulin in the same syringe, certain precautions are necessary:

1) It is important to avoid contaminating a vial of one insulin with another insulin. The order of drawing up the insulins may vary from one diabetes clinic to another. Some clinics recommend drawing up clear rapid-acting insulin (Apidra, Humalog or NovoRapid) or short-acting insulin (Humulin® R or Novolin® ge Toronto) before opaque insulin (Humulin® N or Novolin® ge NPH). **Other clinics advise drawing up opaque insulin before clear insulin so that any contamination of the clear by the opaque can be easily detected.**
2) If one insulin is contaminated by another, the contaminated vial must be discarded because there is a risk that its time of action (start, peak, duration) has been modified. Insulin contaminated by another insulin can hinder the control of blood glucose.
3) It is important to always draw up the insulins in the same order; this will help avoid errors.
4) It is generally recommended to avoid mixing insulins from different manufacturers in the same syringe.
5) **Lantus® (glargine) and Levemir® (detemir) insulins must never be mixed with another insulin.**

4. What is involved in preparing and injecting two types of insulin with the same syringe?

There are three steps involved in preparing and injecting two types of insulin with the same syringe.

Preparing the materials for injection

1) **Wash your hands** with soap and water and dry them well.
2) Lay out the **materials**: syringe, insulin vials, alcohol swab, cotton ball.
    - Use a new syringe for each injection.
    - Use vials of insulin stored at room temperature.
3) Check the labels of the vials to make sure you have the right **types of insulin**.
4) Check the **expiry dates** on the labels: the date printed by the manufacturer and the date recorded after the vials were opened (*see the table in chapter 17 on pages 154-155, listing the temperature and maximum storage times recommended by insulin manufacturers*).

Drawing up the insulins

The order of drawing up the insulins may vary from one diabetes clinic to another.

1) **Roll the vial of opaque insulin** between your hands and turn it upside down to mix the suspension well (**do not shake**). Replace the vial and place it on the table.
2) **Disinfect the caps** of the vials of opaque insulin and clear insulin with an alcohol swab.
3) **Inject air into the vial of clear insulin.**
    - Pull back the plunger of the syringe to draw in an amount of air equal to the amount of clear insulin to be injected. Insert the needle in the rubber cap of the clear insulin vial. Inject the air into the vial. Do not touch the insulin or draw any up. Withdraw the needle from the vial.
4) **Inject the air into the vial of opaque insulin.**
    - Pull back the plunger of the syringe to draw in air equal to the amount of opaque insulin to be injected. Insert the needle in the rubber cap of the opaque insulin vial. Inject the air into the vial. Leave the needle in the vial.
5) **Draw up the required dose of opaque insulin.**
    - Turn the opaque insulin vial and the needle upside down. Pull the plunger back slowly to draw up the number of units of opaque insulin to be injected. Withdraw the needle from the vial.
    - Make sure there are no air bubbles in the syringe; bubbles may cause a smaller amount of insulin to be injected.

      ◦ Push and pull the plunger until the bubbles disappear.

      ◦ Check the syringe to make sure no insulin has been lost; if there has, repeat this step.

6) **Draw up the required dose of clear insulin.**

      ◦ Turn the clear insulin vial upside down. Insert the needle in the rubber cap of the clear insulin vial. Do not introduce any opaque insulin into the clear insulin vial. Pull the plunger back slowly to draw up the number of units of clear insulin to be injected. Withdraw the needle from the vial.

           If you have drawn up too much clear insulin:
- **discard** the insulin drawn up, but save the syringe;
- **start** the process again, from the beginning.

           If the vial of clear insulin is contaminated by opaque insulin:
- **discard** the vial of clear insulin;
- **start** the process again from the beginning with a new vial.

Injecting the insulins and recording the data

1) **Choose the injection area.**

      ◦ Avoid injecting insulin into a limb or part of the body used for any physical activity (for example, a thigh if you intend to take a walk, an arm if you intend to play tennis, etc.).

2) **Choose the injection site** in the area, paying attention to the condition of the skin.

      ◦ Avoid any crease, bump, growth, bruise, blotch or painful spot.

3) **Wash the skin** with soapy water, rinse and let dry.

      ◦ Make sure the injection site is clean. The use of alcohol at home is optional.

4) **Pinch the skin between the thumb and forefinger and keep it pinched** until the end of the injection.

5) Hold the syringe like a pencil and **pierce the skin**.

      ◦ The insulin should be injected into subcutaneous tissue (tissue beneath the skin).

6) **Inject all of the insulin**, pushing the plunger all the way.

      ◦ **Do not pull the plunger back:** raising the plunger to check whether the injection is at the right spot can damage the skin.

      ◦ **Leave the needle in place** for about **5 seconds.**

7) **Withdraw the needle** and carefully press the cotton ball to the injection site.

8) **Record the number of insulin units** injected as well as the type of insulin in the appropriate column of the self-monitoring logbook.

5. What different types of pen-injectors are currently available?

There are several models of pen injectors available (list revised as of January 1st 2009):

Pen-injectors	Manufacturers	Cartridges	Graduation	Dosage dial
Huma Pen® Luxura HD	Eli Lilly Canada Inc.	3 mL	0.5 units at a time	0.5 to 30 units
HumaPen® Luxura	Eli Lilly Canada Inc.	3 mL	1 unit at a time	1 to 60 units
Humulin® N Pen (disposable)	Eli Lilly Canada Inc.	3 mL	1 unit at a time	1 to 60 units
Humalog® Pen (disposable)	Eli Lilly Canada Inc.	3 mL	1 unit at a time	1 to 60 units
Humalog® Mix 25 Pen (disposable)	Eli Lilly Canada Inc.	3 mL	1 unit at a time	1 to 60 units
Novolin-Pen® Junior	Novo Nordisk Canada Inc.	3 mL	0.5 units at a time	0.5 to 35 units
Novolin-Pen® 4	Novo Nordisk Canada Inc.	3 mL	1 unit at a time	1 to 60 units
Autopen® 24 (green)	sanofi aventis Canada Inc.	3 mL	1 unit at a time	1 to 21 units
Autopen® 24 (blue)	sanofi aventis Canada Inc.	3 mL	2 units at a time	2 to 42 units
Apidra® SoloStar (disposable)	sanofi aventis Canada Inc.	3 mL	1 unit at a time	1 to 80 units
Lantus® SoloStar (disposable)	sanofi aventis Canada Inc.	3 mL	1 unit at a time	1 to 80 units

- Check the product monograph for the type of insulin and the type of needle that can be used with the pen-injector selected.
- If using two types of insulin which have not been premixed, you may use two pen-injectors.

6.   How do you prepare for insulin injection with a pen-injector?

The preparation and injection of insulin with a pen-injector involves three steps.

Preparing the materials

1)   **Wash your hands** with soap and water and dry them well.
2)   Lay out the **materials**: pen-injector, insulin cartridge, needle, alcohol swab.
     - Use a new needle for each injection.
     - Use an insulin cartridge stored at room temperature.
3)   Check the **type of insulin and the quantity of insulin** remaining in the cartridge.
4)   Check the expiry dates on the label: the ones printed by the manufacturer and the ones recorded after the cartridges were opened (*see the table in chapter 17 on page 154-155, listing the temperatures and maximum storage time recommended by insulin manufacturers*).
     - Do not refrigerate the pen-injector; cold temperatures can damage it or cause air bubbles to form in the cartridge.
     - Do not share a pen-injector with anyone else.

Selecting a dose of insulin

1)   **Bring opaque insulin to a uniform appearance.** Roll the pen between your palms about ten times to loosen the insulin from the sides, then turn the pen-injector over the same number of times. There is a glass marble inside the opaque insulin cartridge that slides from one end to the other to mix the insulin. Do not shake the pen vigorously, as this could harm the insulin and reduce its effectiveness.
2)   **Screw the needle onto the pen and fill up the empty space in the needle** by selecting one unit of insulin at a time until a drop of insulin appears at the tip of the needle when pointed upwards.
3)   **Select the insulin dose** by turning the dosage ring to the desired number of units.

Injecting the insulin and recording the data

1)   **Choose the injection area.**
     - Avoid injecting insulin into a limb or part of the body used for any physical activity (for example, a thigh if you intend to take a walk, an arm if you intend to play tennis, etc.).
2)   **Choose the injection site** in the area, paying attention to the condition of the skin.
     - Avoid any crease, bump, growth, bruise, blotch or painful spot.
3)   **Disinfect the skin** with an alcohol swab and let it dry.
     - Make sure the injection site is clean. The use of alcohol at home is optional.

4) **Pinch the skin between the thumb and forefinger and keep it pinched** until the end of the injection with **needles measuring 8 mm to 12 mm.**

5) It is generally recommended not to pinch the skin when using **shorter needles (5 mm).**

6) Hold the pen injector like a pencil and **pierce the skin.**

   o The insulin should be injected into subcutaneous tissue (tissue beneath the skin).

7) **Inject all of the insulin,** pushing the plunger down all the way.

   o Leave the needle in place for about 15 seconds.

8) **Withdraw the needle** and carefully press the cotton ball to the injection

   o **Remove** the needle from the pen-injector when the injection is complete. Discard the needle.

9) **Record the number of insulin units** injected as well as the type of insulin in the appropriate column of the self-monitoring logbook.

7. What are the recommended insulin injection techniques?

Insulin should be injected into subcutaneous tissue (the tissue beneath the skin).

1) The proper techniques for injecting insulin are a **subject of controversy.**

2) To ensure a personalized insulin injection technique, it should be chosen with the help of a **health professional.** Several factors have to be taken into account, including age (child or adult) and weight (thin or obese). The length of the needle, the need to pinch the skin, and the angle of injection can vary from person to person.

   o **Most people can reach subcutaneous tissue by injecting at a 90° angle.** However, **thin people or children** may need to pinch the skin, use short needles or inject at a 45° angle to avoid injecting into muscle tissue, especially in the thigh.

   o **Blood** at the injection site can indicate that a muscle has been penetrated. If this occurs, injections should be done at a 45° angle or with short needles (5 mm and 6 mm).

   o A **white area** appearing when the needle is withdrawn can indicate that the insulin has not been injected deeply enough.

   o When the technique requires injection into a **cutaneous fold**, pinch the skin between the thumb and forefinger and keep it pinched until the injection is finished.

    o   Blood glucose levels must be checked more carefully if a **change is made from a long needle to a short needle**. Insulin absorption must remain at the same level.

3) There have not yet been any studies concerning the maximum subcutaneous insulin dose that can be administered at one site. Several factors have to be taken into account, such as the volume of insulin injected at once, the method of injection, the speed of insulin absorption and pain at the injection site.

    o   **In some cases it is recommended that the dose be distributed between two injection sites to make absorption easier.**

    o   One of the factors affecting the speed of subcutaneous insulin is the volume injected. The greater the volume of insulin, the more slowly it is absorbed, and the longer it will take before noticeable absorption begins.

    o   Studies have shown that in most cases, pain at the injection site increases when the volume injected is greater than 50 units.

8. What should be done with used prefilled disposable pen injectors, syringes, needles and lancets?

A system for the disposal of used prefilled disposable pen injectors, syringes, needles and lancets has been implemented to ensure that these items are not left in inappropriate places and cause accidents.

Ideally, special containers that may be obtained for free in pharmacies and in Community Health Centres should be used for disposal. Once filled, the container may be brought to one of four places for disposal: a pharmacy, a Community Health Centre, a diabetes clinic or a participating community organization. If no special containers are available, the used material may be placed in a safely sealed plastic container for disposal.

Insulin Injection: Injection Site Rotation

1. **What part of the body is the best place to inject insulin?**
   Insulin can be injected in different regions of the body. There are eight standard **"injection areas"**:

Areas 1 and 2	**Abdomen:**	right and left sides, except for 2.5 cm (1 inch) around the belly button
Areas 3 and 4	**Arms:**	antero-external surface
Areas 5 and 6	**Thighs:**	antero-external surface
Areas 7 and 8	**Buttocks:**	fleshy upper parts

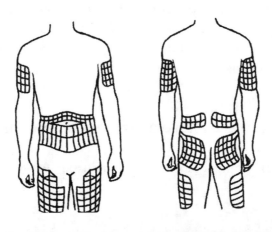

Unless it is possible to fold the skin (create a cutaneous fold), injecting into the distended abdomen of a pregnant woman can damage the skin and is not recommended.

2. How many injection sites are there in each area?

There are a number of places within each **injection area**, known as "**injection sites**", where insulin can be injected. The entire surface of each area can be used, as long as the same injection site **is not used more than once a month**.

3. What distance should there be between injection sites within the same area?

Within the same area, each **injection site** must be at least 1 cm (1/2 inch) from the site of the previous injection:

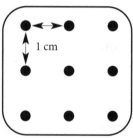

Injection sites

4. Why should a new site be used for each injection?

Injection sites should be rotated **for each insulin injection** to prevent **lipodystrophy** (bumps and cracks from repeated injections at the same site). Not only are these subcutaneous deformations unattractive, more importantly, they hamper the absorption of insulin and the proper control of blood glucose.

5. Does the injection area have an impact on the absorption of the insulin injected?

Yes. The speed of absorption of any one type of insulin varies according to the injection area used.

Insulin is absorbed most quickly in the abdomen, followed by the arms, thighs and buttocks, in that order.

> **Speed of absorption: abdomen > arms > thighs > buttocks**
>
> > = greater than

6. What other factors influence the speed of insulin absorption?

Intense exercise increases the rate of absorption if the insulin is injected into the part of the body being exercised.

- o   For example, insulin injected into your thigh is absorbed more quickly if you take a walk or play tennis afterwards.

Other factors such as heat (sun, bath, etc.), the depth of the injection, or massage near the site can affect the speed of absorption.

7. How can the amount of insulin absorbed be maintained at a stable level despite injection site rotation?

To ensure that the amount of insulin absorbed varies as little as possible, the following steps should be taken:

1) Inject rapid-acting and short-acting insulin into the **abdomen**, either alone or mixed with intermediate-acting insulin. Change the injection site each time.
2) For greater convenience, regularly inject rapid-acting or short-acting insulin into the **arm** before lunch. This will ensure that the peak effect of the midday injection will be more or less the same every day, allowing dosages for this time of day to be adjusted accordingly.
3) To ensure that absorption is as slow as possible, inject intermediate-acting or long-acting insulin that is not mixed with rapid-acting or short-acting insulin into the **thigh or buttocks**.
4) If several injections are administered at different times of the day, the same injection area should be used at the same time every day.
5) A particular area (taking into account speed of absorption) should be used for a given insulin (taking into account time of action) according to the time of injection (taking into account activity level).

6) Lantus® (glargine) and Levemir® (detemir) insulins are long-acting and can meet basal insulin needs with one daily injection. Sometimes two injections are necessary. These insulins are usually injected in areas of slow absorption, such as the thigh. The speed of absorption of Lantus, however, is the same regardless of the area of injection.

In summary:

TYPE OF INSULIN	SUGGESTED AREAS OF INSULIN INJECTION		
	Abdomen	Arm	Thighs and buttocks
Rapid-acting or short-acting, alone	Preferable	Before lunch, for greatest convenience	–
Rapid-acting or short-acting mixed with intermediate-acting	Preferable	–	–
Intermediate-acting, alone	–	–	Preferable
Long-acting, alone	–	–	Preferable

Storage of Insulin

1. Why should precautions be taken when storing insulin?

Insulin is fragile. To ensure that they do not lose their effectiveness, insulin solutions should be stored according to the manufacturers' recommendations. Using improperly stored insulin can impair blood glucose control.

2. What precautions should be taken when storing insulin?

1) Insulin that is **currently in use** can be stored for up to **one month at room temperature**. Injecting cold insulin can cause pain at the injection site.
2) **Reserve supplies** of insulin should be kept in the **refrigerator**. If stored this way, the insulin will remain usable until the expiry date indicated by the manufacturer.
3) Insulin should never be exposed to direct sunlight or heat. Although the product will not necessarily change in appearance, if it is exposed to excessive heat it must be discarded.
4) Insulin should never be frozen. Although the product will not necessarily change in appearance, if it freezes it must also be discarded.
5) A pen injector must not be stored in the refrigerator; this could damage it or create air bubbles in the cartridge. Reserve supplies of insulin in preloaded disposable pen must be kept in refrigerator.
6) Spare insulin syringes that have been prepared in advance should be kept in the refrigerator in an upright or slightly slanted position, with the needle (and its cap) pointing upwards. This will prevent insulin particles from clogging the needle.
7) The date the insulin was opened should be written in the space provided for this purpose on the container.
8) There should always be a reserve of insulin stored in the refrigerator for an emergency, such as breakage.

3. What are some specific recommendations for storing insulin?

The following table shows the temperatures and storage times recommended by insulin manufacturers, listed by the format and brands they sell.

Format	Brand	Recommended temperature	Maximum storage length
Unopened vial or cartridge	Apidra® Humulin® Humalog®	2 °C-8 °C	Expiry date on container
	Novolin® NovoRapid® NovoMix®	2 °C -10 °C	Expiry date on container
	Lantus® Levemir®	2 °C -8 °C	Expiry date on container
Opened vial	Apidra®	15 °C -25 °C (max. 25 °C)	1 month
	Humulin®	18 °C -25 °C (max. 25 °C)	1 month
	Humalog®	18 °C -25 °C (max. 30 °C)	1 month
	Novolin®	18 °C -25 °C (max. 25 °C)	1 month
	NovoRapid®	18 °C -25 °C (max. 37 °C)	1 month
	NovoMix®	18 °C -25 °C (max. 30 °C)	1 month
	Lantus®	15 °C-30 °C (max. 30 °C)	1 month
Opened cartridge	Humulin®	18 °C -25 °C (max. 25 °C)	1 month
	Humalog®	18 °C -25 °C (max. 30 °C)	1 month
	Novolin® NovoRapid®	18 °C -25 °C (max. 37 °C)	1 month
	Lantus®	15 °C -30 °C (max. 30 °C)	1 month
	Levemir®	18 °C -25 °C (max. 30 °C)	42 days

Format	Brand	Recommended temperature	Maximum storage length
Unopened preloaded disposable pen injector	Apidra® SoloSTAR Humulin® N Pen Lantus® SoloSTAR	2°C - 8°C	Expiry date on container
	Humalog® Pen Humalog® Mix 25 Pen	2°C - 10°C	Expiry date on container
Opened preloaded disposable pen injector	Apidra® SoloStar Humulin® N Pen	15°C - 25°C (max. 25°C)	1 month
	Humalog® Pen	18°C - 25°C (max. 30°C)	1 month
	Humalog® Mix 25	18°C - 25°C (max. 30°C)	1 month
	Lantus® SoloSTAR	15°C - 30°C (max. 30°C)	1 month
Syringe, prepared in advance*	Humulin® Humalog®	2°C - 8°C	3 weeks
	Novolin® NovoRapid®	2°C - 10°C	Use as quickly as possible

* It is not recommended to prepare insulin syringes in advance when using Lantus® because it becomes foggy, Apidra or Levemir® because of a lack of data regarding its stability.

4. What should insulin look like?

Insulin comes either in a clear solution that resembles water or in a cloudy suspension that is milky in appearance.

Clear Insulin		Cloudy Insulin	
Rapid:	Apidra® Humalog® NovoRapid®	Intermediate:	Humulin® N Novolin® ge NPH
Short:	Humulin® R Novolin® ge Toronto	Premixed:	Humulin® 30/70 Humalog® Mix 25 Humalog® Mix 50 Novolin® ge 30/70 Novolin® ge 40/60 Novolin® ge 50/50 NovoMix® 30
Long:	Lantus® Levemir®		

5. When should clear insulin be discarded?

Clear insulin should be discarded if:

- o   it looks cloudy;
- o   it is thick;
- o   the solution contains solid particles;
- o   it has been exposed to extreme temperatures (heat or cold);
- o   the recommended expiry date has passed.

6. What precautions should be taken with cloudy insulin?

Cloudy insulin is a suspension that needs to be **mixed well** before being used.

A whitish deposit at the bottom of the vial or in the cartridge is normal, but it must be remixed into the suspension. The vial should be rolled between the palms and turned upside down, or the cartridge should be turned over in the pen injector several times. **Do not shake.**

Improperly mixed cloudy insulin can hamper the precision of measured insulin doses.

7. When should cloudy insulin be discarded?

Cloudy insulin should be discarded if:

- a deposit remains at the bottom of the vial or in the cartridge;
- there are specks floating in the insulin;
- particles are stuck to the sides of the vial or cartridge, making the containers look frosty;
- it has been exposed to extreme temperatures (heat or cold);
- the expiry date has passed.

Insulin Dose Adjustment

1. Why do insulin doses need to be adjusted?

The goal of insulin dose adjustment is to improve the control of blood glucose levels. Ideally, a person with diabetes self-adjusts doses after receiving the appropriate information from his or her health care team.

2. What blood glucose levels should be targeted when adjusting insulin doses?

Most people with diabetes should aim for **target blood glucose levels** between 4 mmol/L and 7 mmol/L before meals and between 5 mmol/L and 10 mmol/L two hours after meals. Target glucose levels after the meals should be tailored to the patient. If diabetes control is not optimal (glycated hemoglobin more than 7% or 0.070) target blood glucose level should be between 5 mmol/L and 8 mmol/L.

3. What are the rules governing insulin dose adjustment?

The following rules are a guide to making safe decisions about insulin dose adjustment. The basic principles are the following:

- o   insulin lowers blood glucose levels;
- o   current blood glucose reflects what happened before.

Before any insulin dose adjustment, time must be taken to analyze blood glucose levels by taking the average of the last three readings for each period of the day (morning, noon, evening and bedtime), going back a maximum of seven days. Only levels recorded since the last adjustment should be considered.

The six suggested rules for adjusting insulin doses are the following:

1) The calculation of the average should not take into account any measurement below 4 mmol/L or above 7 mmol/L that is associated with a **situation that is isolated, exceptional or explainable.**

2) Never adjust insulin doses based on only **one blood glucose test.** Generally speaking, adjusting an insulin dose to correct blood glucose at one given moment is not recommended.

3) Always adjust **only one insulin dose** at a time, at one time of day.

4) Correct **hypoglycemia** first, starting with the first of the day, then the second, etc.
   ○ **Hypoglycemia** can be identified by the following:
      • the average is below 4 mmol/L for a given period of the day;
      • even if the average for a given time of day is greater than or equal to 4 mmol/L, the last two readings or three non-consecutive readings over the last seven days have revealed hypoglycemia.
   ○ A value of 2 mmol/L is assigned to any hypoglycemia that has not been measured.
   ○ A hypoglycemic reading taken outside the four usual blood glucose measuring periods should be recorded for the following period (for example, a hypoglycemic reading measured in the morning should be recorded in the "before lunch" column).

5) Next, correct **hyperglycemia**, that is, when average blood glucose at a given time of day is higher than 7 mmol/L. Begin with the first episode of the day, then the next, and so on.
   ○ Watch out for **rebound hyperglycemia**. Rebound hyperglycemia is a blood glucose reading **above** 7 mmol/L that follows hypoglycemia. This type of hyperglycemia should not be considered when calculating the average. Nocturnal hypoglycemia can cause rebound hyperglycemia upon waking. When in doubt, take a blood glucose reading around 2 a.m. and if necessary correct the hypoglycaemia instead of the morning hyperglycemia.

6) It is recommended to wait at least two days after an adjustment before making any new modifications. The only exception is when there are two consecutive nocturnal or morning hypoglycemic readings, in which case the rule must be disregarded and the dose of insulin that caused it must be decreased.

4. What are the most frequently prescribed insulin regimens?

There are a number of different insulin regimens. The four most commonly prescribed are the following.

1) The **split-mixed regimen** involves injecting one intermediate-acting insulin (e.g. Humulin® N or Novolin® ge NPH) and one rapid-acting (Apidra®, Humalog® or NovoRapid®) or short-acting insulin (Humulin® R or Novolin® ge Toronto) before breakfast and dinner. Sometimes, the injection of intermediate-acting insulin before dinner should be delayed until bedtime to avoid nocturnal hypoglycemia.

2) The **basal-prandial regimen** consists of injecting one rapid-acting (Apidra®, Humalog® or NovoRapid®) or short-acting insulin (Humulin® R or Novolin® ge Toronto) before each meal and one intermediate-acting (for example, Humulin® N or Novolin® ge NPH) or long-acting insulin (Lantus® or Levemir®) at bedtime. Although basal insulin is usually administered in one injection, it can also be administered in more than one injection during the course of the day. The dose of rapid-acting or short-acting insulin can be fixed (fixed carbohydrate regimen) or measured according to the amount of carbohydrates consumed in a meal (variable carbohydrate regimen). In the variable carbohydrate regimen the dose is determined according to a ratio, such as 1 unit: 10 g of carbohydrates, that is, 1 unit of insulin per 10 g of carbohydrates consumed.

3) The **premixed regimen** involves injecting one premixed insulin (for example, Humulin® 30/70, Novolin® ge 50/50, Humalog® Mix 25, NovoMix®30, etc.) before breakfast and dinner.

4) The **combined regimen** involves injecting one intermediate-acting insulin (Humulin® N or Novolin® ge NPH) or long-acting insulin (Lantus® and Levemir®) at bedtime, in addition to oral antidiabetic drugs during the day.

5. In the split-mixed regimen, which insulins affect blood glucose levels during the day?

Insulin	affects	blood glucose levels measured
Intermediate-acting before dinner	⟶	before breakfast
Rapid-acting or short-acting before breakfast	⟶	before lunch
Intermediate-acting before breakfast	⟶	before dinner
Rapid-acting or short-acting before dinner	⟶	at bedtime (before the snack)

Blood glucose levels at any given moment reflect the action of the previous insulin injection.

6. How should insulin doses be adjusted in the split-mixed regimen?

In general, when **hypoglycemia (average blood glucose below 4 mmol/L)** occurs before meals and at bedtime (as defined in the adjustment rules), the insulin dose should be **decreased** by two units at a time. If the **total daily dose** of insulin is less than or equal to 20 units, the dose that caused it should be reduced by one unit at a time.

In general, when **hyperglycemia (average blood glucose above 7 mmol/L)** occurs before meals and at bedtime (as defined in the adjustment rules), the insulin dose should be **increased** by two units at a time. If the **total daily dose** of insulin is less than or equal to 20 units, the dose that caused it should be increased by one unit at a time.

It is recommended to wait at least two days after any insulin dose adjustment before making any new changes. In the event of hypoglycemia or hyperglycemia, the insulin dose that caused it must be adjusted within one week.

7. **In the basal-prandial regimen, which insulins affect blood glucose levels at different times of day?**

Insulin	affects	blood glucose levels measured
Intermediate- or long-acting at bedtime	⟶	before breakfast
Rapid acting or short acting before breakfast	⟶	before lunch
Rapid-acting or short-acting before lunch	⟶	before dinner
Rapid-acting or short-acting before dinner	⟶	at bedtime (before the snack)

> Blood glucose levels at any given moment reflect the action of the previous insulin injection.

8. **How should insulin doses be adjusted in the basal-prandial with fixed carbohydrate regimen?**

In general, when **hypoglycemia (average blood glucose below 4 mmol/L)** occurs before meals and at bedtime (as defined by the adjustment rules), the insulin dose should be **decreased** by two units at a time. If the **total daily dose** of insulin is less than or equal to 20 units, however, the dose that caused it should be reduced by one unit at a time.

In general, when **hyperglycemia (average blood glucose above 7 mmol/L)** occurs before meals and at bedtime (as defined by the adjustment rules), the insulin dose should be **increased** by two units at a time. If the **total daily dose** of insulin is less than or equal to 20 units, however, the dose that caused it should be increased by one unit at a time.

It is recommended to wait at least two days after an insulin dose adjustment before making any new changes. The only exception is when two consecutive episodes of hypoglycemia occur during the same period, in which case the rule must be disregarded and the dose of insulin that caused it must be decreased. In the event of hypoglycemia or hyperglycemia, the insulin dose that caused it must be adjusted within one week.

9. **How should insulin doses be adjusted in the basal-prandial with variable carbohydrate regimen?**

When **hypoglycemia (average blood glucose below 4 mmol/L)**, as defined by the rules of adjustment, occurs:

1) during the night or before breakfast, the dose of intermediate-acting (for example, Humulin® N or Novolin® ge NPH) or long-acting insulin (Lantus® or Levemir®) must be decreased by two units at a time. If the daily dose of intermediate-acting or long-acting insulin is less than or equal to 10 units, however, the dose should be decreased by only one unit at a time;

2) before lunch, dinner or bedtime, the dose of insulin that caused it (Apidra®, Humalog®, NovoRapid®, Humulin® R or Novolin® ge Toronto) must be **decreased** by 0.2 units/10 g of carbohydrates. If the dose of insulin is less than or equal to 0.5 units/10 g of carbohydrates, however, the dose should be decreased by only 0.1 unit/10 g of carbohydrates at a time.

If **hyperglycemia (average blood glucose above 7 mmol/L)**, as defined by the rules of adjustment, occurs:

1) during the night or before breakfast, the dose of intermediate acting (for example, Humulin® N or Novolin® ge NPH) or long acting insulin (Lantus® or Levemir®) should be increased by two units at a time. If the daily dose of intermediate acting or long acting insulin is less than or equal to 10 units, however, the dose should be increased by only one unit at a time;

2) before lunch, dinner or bedtime, the dose of insulin that caused it (Apidra®, Humalog®, NovoRapid®, Humulin® R or Novolin® ge Toronto) must be increased by 0.2 units/10 g of carbohydrates. If the dose of insulin is less than or equal to 0.5 units/10 g of carbohydrates, the dose should be increased by only 0.1 unit/10 g of carbohydrates at a time.

It is recommended to wait at least two days after an insulin dose adjustment before making any new changes. The only exception is when two consecutive episodes of hypoglycemia occur during the same period, in which case the rule must be disregarded and the dose of insulin that caused it must be decreased. In the event of hypoglycemia or hyperglycemia, the insulin dose that caused it must be adjusted within one week.

10. In the premixed regimen, which insulins affect blood glucose levels at different times of day?

Premixed insulin	affects	blood glucose levels measured
Rapid-acting or short-acting and intermediate-acting insulin before breakfast	⟶	before lunch and before dinner
Rapid-acting or short-acting and intermediate-acting insulin before dinner	⟶	at bedtime (before the snack) and before breakfast

Blood glucose levels at any given moment reflect the action of the previous insulin injection.

11. How should insulin doses be adjusted in the premixed regimen?

In general, when **hypoglycemia (average blood glucose below 4 mmol/L)** as defined by the adjustment rules occurs before meals and at bedtime, the mixed insulin dose that caused it should be **decreased** by two units at a time. If the **total daily dose** of insulin is less than or equal to 20 units, however, the dose should be reduced by only one unit at a time.

In general, when **hyperglycemia (average blood glucose above 7 mmol/L)** as defined by the adjustment rules occurs, the mixed insulin dose that caused it should be **increased** by two units at a time. If the **total daily dose** of insulin is less than or equal to 20 units, the dose should be increased by only one unit at a time.

It should be recalled that premixed insulins are responsible for two periods of the day at a time. Consequently, if there is a difference between blood glucose at bedtime and in the morning (for example, elevated at bedtime and low in the morning) or between blood glucose before lunch and before dinner, **a doctor should be consulted, as this could mean that the mixture has to be changed.**

It is recommended to wait at least two days after an insulin dose adjustment before making any new changes. In the event of hypoglycemia or hyperglycemia, the insulin dose that caused it must be adjusted within one week

12. In the combined regimen, which blood glucose reading is affected by insulin administered at bedtime?

In the combined regimen, **morning blood glucose** is affected by intermediate acting or long acting insulin administered at bedtime.

13. How should insulin doses be adjusted in the combined regimen?

In general, when morning **hypoglycemia (average blood glucose below 4 mmol/L)** as defined by the adjustment rules occurs, the bedtime insulin dose should be **decreased** by two units at a time. If the total daily dose of insulin is less than or equal to 10 units, however, the dose should be reduced by only one unit.

In general, when morning **hyperglycemia (average blood glucose above 7 mmol/L)** as defined by the adjustment rules occurs, the bedtime insulin dose must be **increased** by two units at a time. If the total daily dose of insulin is less than or equal to 10 units, however, the dose should be increased by one unit.

It is recommended to wait at least two days after an insulin dose adjustment before making any new changes. In the event of hypoglycemia or hyperglycemia, the insulin dose that caused it must be adjusted within one week.

Practical Examples

It is important to understand the rules of adjustment described in this chapter before attempting any insulin dose adjustment. The following practical examples can be useful:

Example 1

Treatment: Split-mixed regimen:

Humulin® R	12 units at breakfast and 10 units at dinner
Humulin® N	20 units at breakfast and 14 units at dinner
Total daily dose of insulin = 56 units	

Self-monitoring logbook:

	Blood Glucose			
Date	**Before breakfast (mmol/L)**	**Before lunch (mmol/L)**	**Before dinner (mmol/L)**	**At bedtime (mmol/L)**
16/05	6.4	7.7	6.5	5.7
17/05	7.1	9.3	7.0	5.4
18/05	5.9	7.5	6.2	6.0
Average	6.5	8.2	6.6	5.7

Analysis:

In this example, blood glucose levels before lunch are above 7 mmol/L (hyperglycemia). The appropriate adjustment is to increase the morning dose of short-acting insulin by two units.

Example 2

Treatment: basal-prandial with fixed carbohydrate regimen:

NovoRapid®	8 units at breakfast, 6 units at lunch, 6 units at dinner
Novolin® ge NPH	16 units at bedtime
Total daily dose of insulin = 36 units	

Self-monitoring logbook:

Date	Blood Glucose			
	Before breakfast (mmol/L)	Before lunch (mmol/L)	Before dinner (mmol/L)	At bedtime (mmol/L)
03/01	12.0	9.0	8.0	6.5
04/01	13.0	8.7	7.2	5.8
05/01	11.7	8.9	7.8	5.6
Average	12.2	8,.9	7.7	6.0

Analysis:

In this example, hyperglycemia occurs before breakfast, lunch and dinner. The first hyperglycemia of the day, the one occurring before breakfast, should be corrected first. To do so, the NPH insulin taken at bedtime should be **increased** by 2 units to 18 units. It is still a good idea to **check blood glucose** at 2 a.m., however, to ensure there is no nocturnal hypoglycemia that could cause rebound hyperglycemia in the morning. If nocturnal hypoglycemia does occur, the bedtime dose of NPH insulin should be **decreased** by 2 units.

Example 3

Treatment: basal-prandial with variable carbohydrate regimen:

Apidra®	1.2 units/10 g of carbohydrates at breakfast
	1.0 unit/10 g of carbohydrates at lunch
	0.8 units/10 g of carbohydrates at dinner
Lantus®	12 units at bedtime

Self-monitoring logbook:

Date	Blood Glucose			
	Before breakfast (mmol/L)	Before lunch (mmol/L)	Before dinner (mmol/L)	At bedtime (mmol/L)
13/04	5.4	6.4	4.4	5.8
14/04	5.9	6.0	3.6	5.0
15/04	5.3	5.6	2.8	5.2
Average	5.5	6.0	3.6	5.3

Analysis:

In this example, two episodes of **hypoglycemia** are detected in the last two blood glucose readings taken before dinner. The appropriate adjustment is to **decrease** the insulin dose before lunch by 0.2 units/10 g of carbohydrates, or in other words, from 1.0 unit/10 g to 0.8 units/10 g of carbohydrates.

The Insulin Pump:
Another Treatment Option

1. What is an insulin pump?

An insulin pump is a device consisting of:
1) a reservoir or cartridge containing insulin;
2) an electric motor to inject insulin from the reservoir;
3) a catheter (cannula) attached to the insulin reservoir and equipped with a small needle that is inserted beneath the skin of the abdomen, where the insulin is injected.

An insulin pump administers insulin subcutaneously on a continual basis, 24 hours a day; this is called the **basal rate**. The basal rate fills all insulin needs regardless of meals (basal dose). The pump can be programmed to provide different basal rates to meet insulin needs that vary according to the time of day. Before meals, an extra dose is injected via the pump to meet insulin needs associated with meals; this is called the **bolus dose**. The continual release of insulin along with the pre-meal bolus imitates the normal function of the pancreas.

Generally, insulin pumps use rapid-acting insulin such as Apidra®, Humalog® or NovoRapid®.

The insulin pump is not an artificial pancreas. It does only what it is programmed to do.

2. What are the indications for using an insulin pump?

Current indications for using an insulin pump tend to be restrictive because the equipment is expensive. The following indications are usually recognized:

1) serious hypoglycemia (requiring the help of a third person) on more than one occasion (two or more over the last twelve months);
2) great blood glucose lability (instability) requiring repeated medical attention (two or more hospitalizations over the last twelve months);
3) inadequate control of blood glucose (glycosylated hemoglobin $\geq$ 8%) despite an attempt at intensive insulinotherapy;
4) accelerated progression of complications (retinopathy and/or neuropathy) with sub-optimal control of blood glucose (glycosylated hemoglobin > 7%).

The insulin pump can also be an option in the following situations:
1) pregnancy;
2) a request from a diabetic person who wants to intensify treatment;
3) a person with a very irregular schedule or very active lifestyle.

3. How much does insulin pump treatment cost?

An insulin pump costs approximately $6,500, and the materials required (needles, catheters, insulin, etc.) can cost between $2,000 and $4,000 a year.

4. Is insulin pump treatment covered by medical insurance?

No. Provincial medical insurance does not cover the purchase cost of an insulin pump or the materials required. Some private insurance companies, however, will cover up to 80% of the costs if the justification for this type of treatment is accepted. Other companies will contribute a maximum, non-renewable amount.

5. What should I do if I think I could benefit from insulin pump treatment?

First, discuss it with your endocrinologist. If insulin pump treatment is appropriate, you must:
1) check with your insurance company to see whether it covers insulin pump treatment costs;
2) get the following from your doctor:
    o a prescription for an insulin pump;
    o a letter justifying the indication for insulin pump treatment, to be submitted to your insurance company.

6. What procedures should be followed when using an insulin pump?

Using an insulin pump requires instruction from a qualified health care team.

An endocrinologist prescribes and adjusts insulin doses. The instructions received should include:
1) how the pump functions;
2) how to install the catheter and how to choose the injection area;
3) how to calculate carbohydrates;

The endocrinologist will provide information about the procedures to follow and the people to contact.

7. How is insulin pump dosage determined?

Generally, rapid-acting insulin (Apidra®, Humalog® or NovoRapid®) is used. To determine the **basal dose**, begin with 50% of the total insulin dose for the day according to prior treatment (for example, total dose for 24 hours = 40 units, so 40 ÷ 2 = 20 units for the basal dose). When determining the daily distribution of the basal dose, the two following two points must be considered: 1) generally speaking, people are most sensitive to insulin between midnight and 4 a.m. and are therefore the most vulnerable to hypoglycemia during these hours; 2) people are generally most resistant to insulin between 4 a.m. to 8 a.m and therefore more insulin is required during this period. The midnight basal rate should therefore be decreased by 25% and the 4 a.m. rate increased by 25-50%.

For example, if the amount of insulin is 20 units per 24 hours, the basal rate is 0.8 units/hour (20 units ÷ 24 hours = 0.8 units/hour). However, when the information above is taken into account, the basal rate can be decreased by 25% between midnight and 4 a.m. (to 0.6 units/hour) and increased by 50% between 4 a.m. and 8 a.m. (to 1.2 units/hour).

To determine the **pre-meal bolus insulin dose**, begin with 1.0 unit per 10 g of carbohydrates for each meal, then adjust the dose as needed. For example, a meal containing 60g of carbohydrates requires a dose of 6 units: (60 g ÷ 10 g) x 1.0 unit = 6 units.

8. Are there always different basal rates for different times of day?

Not necessarily. However, there are five distinct periods in a day and it is possible for basal requirements to vary with each one

> **Period 1:** 12 a.m. (midnight) – 4 a.m. People are most vulnerable to hypoglycemia during these hours and it may be necessary to deliver less insulin.

> **Period 2:** 4 a.m. – 8 a.m. People are more insulin-resistant during this period and may need more insulin

> **Period 3:** 8 a.m. – 12 p.m. (noon). This is a more active period of the day and may require a lower basal rate.

> **Period 4:** 12 p.m. (noon) – 6 p.m. This is a more active period of the day and may require a lower basal rate.

> **Period 5:** 6 p.m. – 12 a.m. (midnight). This less active period may require a higher basal rate.

9. Which blood glucose readings are used to adjust the basal rate?

It is important to identify the blood glucose readings during the day that reflect the basal rate for each period. These readings can be used as a basis for making adjustments.

Period	Basal blood glucose
Midnight to 4 a.m.	2 a.m.
4 to 8 a.m.	before breakfast (around 7-8 a.m.)
8 a.m. to 12 noon	before lunch (around 11 a.m.-noon)
12 noon to 6 p.m.	before dinner (around 4-6 p.m.)
6 p.m. to midnight	bedtime (around 11 p.m.-midnight)

10. Which blood glucose readings are used to adjust the pre-meal bolus dose?

The bolus for each meal is adjusted according to the postprandial blood glucose reading (1-2 hours after the beginning of the meal).

Meal		Postprandial blood glucose (1-2 hours after a meal)
Breakfast	⟶	after breakfast
Lunch	⟶	after lunch
Dinner	⟶	after dinner

11. What are the target blood glucose levels?

Basal blood glucose:

Most people are advised to target a blood glucose level between 4 mmol/L and 7 mmol/L before meals and at bedtime (before the snack).

Postprandial blood glucose:

The recommended postprandial blood glucose level is higher than the pre-meal blood glucose. Most people should aim for a postprandial target blood glucose level between 5 mmol/L and 10 mmol/L (1-2 hours after the beginning of the meal). Target glucose levels after the meals should be tailored to the patient. If diabetes control is not optimal (glycated hemoglobin more than 7% or 0.070) target blood glucose level should be between 5 mmol/L and 8 mmol/L.

12. What are the insulin adjustment rules?

Before insulin doses are adjusted, blood glucose levels should be analyzed by calculating the average of the last two or three readings for each period of the day (before meals, after meals and at bedtime), going back no further than seven days. Only readings done since the last adjustment should be taken into account.

There are six insulin adjustment rules:

1) In the calculation of the average, do not take into account any measurements lower than 4 mmol/L or higher than 7 mmol/L that are associated with an **isolated, exceptional and explainable** situation.

2) Never adjust insulin doses on the basis of only **one blood glucose reading**. Adjusting insulin dosage to correct blood glucose at any one given moment is generally discouraged.

3) Adjust **only one insulin dose** at a time (basal or bolus) and for one time of day only.

4) Correct **hypoglycemia** first, starting with the first of the day.
   - **Basal hypoglycemia** occurs when:
     - the basal blood glucose average for a given period of the day is below 4 mmol/L;
     - the last two readings or two of three non-consecutive hypoglycemic readings taken over the last seven days for the same time of day reveal hypoglycemia, even if the average is equal to or greater than 4 mmol/L.
   - **Postprandial hypoglycemia** occurs when:
     - average postprandial blood glucose levels after a meal are lower than average blood glucose levels before the same meal;
     - the last two postprandial readings or two of three non-consecutive readings over the last seven days for the same meal reveal blood glucose levels lower than before the meal, even if average postprandial blood glucose levels are higher than average blood glucose levels before the meal.
   - Assign a value of 2 mmol/L to any hypoglycemia that has not been measured.
   - Hypoglycemia that occurs outside the usual blood glucose measuring periods should be recorded under the following period (for example, hypoglycemia occurring at 11 a.m. is entered in the "before lunch" column).

5) Next, correct **hyperglycemia**, which occurs when the basal blood glucose level for the same time of day is greater than 7 mmol/L or the postprandial blood glucose level is greater than 10 mmol/L. Begin with the first of the day, followed by the second, and so on.
   - **Watch out for rebound hyperglycemia**. Rebound hyperglycemia is a basal blood glucose level above 7 mmol/L that follows hypoglycemia. This type of hyperglycemia should not be considered when calculating the average.

6) Wait at least two days after adjusting a dose before making any other changes.

13. How should insulin doses be adjusted?

The basal rate is determined according to blood glucose measured at 2 a.m., before meals and at bedtime. The bolus rate is determined according to blood glucose measured 1 or 2 hours after the beginning of the meal. These values are then used to adjust insulin doses as follows:

Basal:
- If hypoglycemic ⟶ decrease the corresponding basal rate by 0.1 unit/hour to 0.2 units/hour.
- If hyperglycemic ⟶ increase the corresponding basal rate by 0.1 unit/hour to 0.2 units/hour.

Bolus:
- If hypoglycemic ⟶ decrease the bolus by 0.1 unit to 0.2 units/ 10 g of carbohydrates.
- If hyperglycemic ⟶ increase the bolus by 0.1 unit to 0.2 unit/10 g of carbohydrates.

14. What types of insulin pumps are available in Canada?

The following table presents a list of the latest generation of insulin pumps currently on market, along with a few of their features (list revised as of January 1st 2009, adapted from a document entitled "Comparaison des pompes à insuline" from the Quebec University Hospital).

MODEL	Accu-Chek® Spirit	Animas® 2020	Cozmo®	Paradigm® • 522 • 722
Manufacturer or distributor	Disetronic Medical Systems Inc.	Johnson & Johnson	Auto Control Médical	Medtronic
Weight of pump (in grams)	79	88	90	100 108
Size (cm)	8.1 x 5.6 x 2.1	7.62 x 5.08 x 2.18	8.8 x 5 x 1.9	8.6 x 5 x 1.8 9.6 x 5 x 1.8
Colour	blue	blue, silver, black, pink and green	blue, black, purple	transparent, smoke, blue, purple
Reservoir	315 units	200 units	300 units	176 units 300 units
Connection	Luer lock	Luer lock	Luer lock	Luer lock Paradigm
Suggested batteries	AA alkaline or rechargeable (1 battery)	AA alkaline or lithium (1 battery)	AAA alkaline (1 battery)	AAA alkaline (1 battery)
Battery lifespan	alkaline (1 month); rechargeable (1 week)	lithium (5-7 weeks) alkaline (2-3 weeks)	1 month	4-6 weeks
Watertightness	60 mins at 2.5 metres	24 hrs at 3.6 metres	3 mins at 3.6 metres or 30 mins at 2.4 metres	30 mins at 1 metre
Base delivery	0.1 to 25 units/hr	0.025 to 25 units/hr	0.05 to 35 units/hr	0.05 to 35 units/hr
Basal release	Every 3 mins	Every 3 mins	Every 3 mins	Total dose administered over 60 minutes in increments or stages of 0.05
Temporary basal rate	0% to 250% 15 mins – 24 hrs	0% to 200% 30 mins – 24 hrs	0% to 250% 30 mins – 72 hrs	0% to 200% 30 mins – 24 hrs
Bolus calculator	On a Palm PDA	yes	yes	yes (touch screen)

MODEL	Accu-Chek® Spirit	Animas® 2020	Cozmo®	Paradigm® • 522 • 722
Bolus	0.1 to 25 units (in increments or stages of 0.1, 0.2, 0.5, 1 and 2)	0.05 to 35 units (increments or stages of 0.05)	0.05 to 75 units (increments or stages of 0.05 – 0.1 – 0.5 – 1 – 2 and 5)	0.1 to 25 units (increments or stages of 0.1)
Length of bolus for 1 unit	5 secs	1 or 4 secs	adjustable 1-5 mins	40 secs
Memory	30 events per categories (bolus, alerts, daily totals, temporary basal rate)	500 bolus, 120 daily totals	4,000 events	90 days (through software) 24 bolus on pump
downloading software	yes Accu-check Smart Pix	yes Ezmanager	yes Cozmanager	yes Carelink Pro software (for professionals) or Carelink Personnal (for patients) or Web site at www.carelink.minimed.com
Blood glucose meter	Aviva or Compact Plus	One Touch model	Cozmonitor Freestyle IR (communicates results in the pump via infrared)	Contour® Link (communicates results in the pump via radio frequency)
Specific features	Bolus calculator on a Palm PDA; 12 languages; reversible screen; tactile buttons; emergency pump	Colour screen Personalized food list with carbohydrates option	Blood glucose meter that attaches to the pump	Continual REAL Time blood glucose system on pump screen Alarms for hypo/hyperglycemia

MODEL	Accu-Chek® Spirit	Animas® 2020	Cozmo®	Paradigm® • 522 • 722
Technical support	1-866-703-3476	1-866-406-4844	1-800-630-0864	1-800-284-4416
Price	$6,395 for pump, Palm PDA and emergency pump	$6,895	$6,500	$6,800 (Minilink Transmitter $700)
Internet address	www.disetronic-ca.com www.accuchek.ca	www.animas.ca	www.autocontrol.com	www.minimed.ca www.medtronic.com

* Prices may vary. Additional material can cost between $2,000 and $4,000 a year.

15. When should the injection site be changed?

1) Immediately:
    o   if you feel pain or discomfort;
    o   if two corrective bolus doses fail to reduce an elevated blood glucose (blocked catheter);
    o   if ketone bodies are present in the blood or urine, for no apparent reason;
    o   if you see blood in the catheter.

2) Every 24 to 48 hours:
    o   if you use a steel needle set;
    o   if you are pregnant.
3) Every 48 to 72 hours:
    o   if you use a flexible cannula set.

It is generally recommended that the **perfusion device (that is, the reservoir, tubing and catheter) be replaced every 48 to 72 hours**. The suggested frequency of replacement varies according to the pump, brand of insulin and type of catheter used.

Physical activity

1. What is physical activity?

Physical activity is defined as any bodily movement produced by the muscles and requiring an expenditure of energy.

2. Why is regular exercise so important?

Regular exercise is beneficial for everyone, whether or not they have diabetes. There are certain risks associated with inactivity.

Regular physical activity leads to the following benefits:
1) better health, improved physical fitness, increased self-esteem;
2) better posture and balance;
3) strengthening of the muscles and bones;
4) energy recovery;
5) weight control;
6) lower blood lipid levels;
7) relaxation and stress control;
8) increased autonomy in later years;

The risks associated with inactivity are the following:
1) early death;
2) heart disease;
3) obesity;
4) high blood pressure;
5) diabetes;
6) osteoporosis;
7) stroke;
8) depression;
9) colon cancer.

3. What are the benefits of a regular exercise program for people with glucose intolerance (pre-diabetic state) or people with diabetes?

People with glucose intolerance and people with diabetes derive the same benefits from exercise as people with normal glucose tolerance. However, people who are glucose intolerant and engage in moderate regular physical activity decrease their risk of developing diabetes. People with type 2 diabetes who engage in regular physical activity decrease their resistance to insulin and are better able to control their diabetes.

Regular exercise is as beneficial for people with type 1 diabetes as it is for people who do not have diabetes. It is vital, however, for people with diabetes to control their illness and adjust insulin doses and diet according to their physical activity.

4. How should a successful exercise program be approached?

1) First, choose a sport or activity that you like. Dancing, mild gymnastics, swimming, working out, and speed-walking are all examples of simple and pleasant physical activities. The important thing is to choose something that appeals to you. This will increase the likelihood that you will do it on a daily basis.

2) Include the activity in your daily schedule. The more physical activity a person engages in every day, the greater his or her sense of well-being. Daily life offers a number of opportunities for exercise:
   o   walking or biking to work;
   o   taking the stairs instead of the elevator;
   o   doing manual tasks such as sweeping, cleaning windows, gardening, etc.

According to recent recommendations, all adults between 18 and 65 years old should have at least **150 minutes of moderate physical activity per week, or 30 minutes, five times a week.**

5. What is considered a good physical fitness program to help control diabetes?

1) The exercises selected require **moderately intense levels of effort**.
2) The person exercises most days of the week, **at least five days a week.**
3) The person exercises an average of **at least 30 minutes a day**. The physical activity can be performed for shorter periods of at least 10 minutes per session.

The most accessible exercise is **speed-walking**. Walking quickly, but at a pace that allows conversation without breathlessness, is considered to be an activity of moderate intensity.

The energy expended by engaging in regular physical activity helps people maintain a healthy weight.

6. What are some low, moderate, and elevated intensity exercises?

The following chart ranks examples of physical activities according to the length and intensity of effort they generally require.

Washing and waxing a car (45-60 mins)	**Less intense**
Washing floors and windows (45-60 mins)	**Longer**
Gardening (30-45 mins)	
Moving around in a wheelchair (30-40 mins)	
Walking 3 km in 35 minutes (12 mins/km)	↑
Dancing (fast, for 30 mins)	
Walking with a baby (2.5 km in 30 mins)	
Raking leaves (30 mins)	
Walking 3.5 km in 30 minutes (8½ mins/km)	
Aqua-fitness (30 mins)	
Swimming (20 mins)	
Biking 6.5 km in 15 minutes	
Running 2.5 km in 15 minutes (6 mins/km)	↓
Shoveling snow or climbing stairs (15 mins)	**More intense**
	Shorter

7. **How can the exercise be pleasurable, effective and safe?**
How can I ensure that I progress at my own speed?

It is strongly recommended that people beginning an exercise program start out slowly and increase their pace little by little. Knowing how to measure out your physical effort is therefore critical and a good way to assess your abilities and progress. There are a number of ways to set your own pace.

1) **The degree of breathlessness:** Find the level where your breathing is deeper than when at rest but you are still able to have a conversation.

2) **Pulse or heart rate (HR):** Exercise is considered moderate when your pulse falls between 50% and 70% of your maximum heart rate. If an exact measurement of your maximum heart rate is not available, it can be estimated by subtracting your age from 220 beats per minute. To determine the moderate zone, this result should be multiplied by 50% or 70%.

   For example, if a person is 45 years old:
   (220 - 45) x 50% = 87.5
   (220 - 45) x 70% = 122.5

Moderate exercise means a heart rate between 88 and 123 beats per minute. This estimate does not, however, take into account drugs that can affect heart rate.

The following table can help you determine whether the intensity is appropriate:

Time needed depends on effort				
Very Light Effort	Light Effort *60 minutes*	Moderate Effort *30-60 minutes*	Vigorous Effort *20-30 minutes*	Maximum Effort
• Strolling • Dusting	• Light walking • Volleyball • Easy gardening • Stretching	• Brisk walking • Biking • Raking leaves • Swimming • Dancing • Water aerobics	• Aerobics • Jogging • Hockey • Basketball • Fast Swimming • Fast aerobics	• Sprinting • Racing
	How does it feel? How warm am I? What is my breathing like?			
• No change from rest state • Normal breathing	• Starting to feel warm • Slight increase in breathing rate	• Warmer • Greater increase in breathing rate	• Quite warm • More out of breath	• Very hot/perspiring heavily • Completely out of breath
Range needed to stay healthy				

Handbook for *Canada's Physical Activity Guide to Healthy Active Living.* Ottawa, Ontario, K1A 0S9.
Tel.: 1-888-334-9769; Website: http://www.phac-aspc.gc.ca/pau-uap/paguide/index.html

3) **The Borg Perceived Effort Scale:** This scale, which measures an individual's subjective perception of his or her effort, is easy to use. It is an excellent way to assess the intensity of physical activity undertaken by people who are taking drugs that affect their heart rate. An intensity of 12-13 corresponds to a moderate level of effort (see illustration below). Although the measurement is subjective, an estimate of perceived effort can provide a fairly reliable assessment of the person's actual heart rate during the physical activity.

The Borg scale should be referred to while the physical effort is taking place. The scale ranges from 6 to 20, with 6 signifying "no effort at all" and 20 signifying "exhaustion" or "maximal effort". Choose the number the best corresponds to your perception of your effort. It will give a good idea of the intensity of your physical activity and will guide you either to accelerate or slow down your movements to achieve the intensity you want. An accurate estimate depends on your being as honest as possible in your evaluation of your exertion.

BORG SCALE
Perceived effort

	6
Extremely light (7.5)	7
	8
Very light	9
	10
Light	11
	12
Somewhat hard	13
	14
Hard	15
	16
Very hard	17
	18
Extremely strenuous	19
	20

8. When is exercise dangerous for people with diabetes?

Exercise can be risky and contraindicated when a person's diabetes is poorly controlled and blood glucose is:

1) lower than 4 mmol/L;
2) above 14.0 mmol/L and there are ketone bodies in the urine or blood;
3) above 17.0 mmol/L, whether or not there are ketone bodies in the urine or blood.

In some cases, people with diabetes can engage in regular physical activity, although they must always make careful choices regarding the type of activity they engage in.

For example:

1) **if the person with diabetes has a heart problem**, he or she should only undertake an exercise program under medical supervision;
2) **if the person with diabetes has eye problems with a risk of hemorrhage**, he or she should take up physical activities such as swimming, walking and riding a stationary bike instead of anaerobic activities such as weightlifting or activities that can involve blows or jolts, such as boxing, racket sports (tennis, badminton) and jogging;
3) **if the diabetic person has serious neuropathy with complete loss of sensation in the feet**, he or she should take up activities such as swimming, biking, rowing, arm exercises or exercises performed while seated.

Generally speaking, walking for short periods remains one of the least risky activities, even in such special cases.

9. What potential risks does exercise present for a person with diabetes who is taking oral antidiabetic medications or insulin?

People with diabetes being treated with insulin or drugs that stimulate the pancreas to produce more insulin (e.g. glyburide, gliclazide, repaglinide) run a higher risk of **hypoglycemia**, especially if the activity is unplanned, prolonged, and of moderate intensity.

It should be remembered that:

1) moderate exercise sustained for several hours can cause delayed hypoglycemia as long as 12 to 16 hours after the activity. For example, cross-country skiing, house-cleaning or even several hours of shopping can all provoke delayed hypoglycemia;

2) the more regular the activity (schedule, duration and intensity), the lower the risk of hypoglycemia.

10. What precautions should be taken when planning to exercise?

1) Blood glucose should be measured **before** any physical activity, regardless of the treatment regimen.
2) The condition of the feet should be checked **before and after** any exercise.
3) Alcohol should not be consumed **before, during or after** exercise.
4) People with diabetes should always wear a diabetic ID bracelet or pendant.
5) People with diabetes should also have quickly metabolized carbohydrate sources on hand.
6) People taking insulin are advised to use an injection site in an area that will be the least involved in the exercise, such as the abdomen.

11. What can people with diabetes who are taking insulin do to prevent hypoglycemia when exercising?

People with diabetes who are taking rapid or short acting insulin before meals should know how to adapt their treatment to prevent hypoglycemia when exercising.

1) When the activity is **planned and takes place 1 to 2 hours after a meal**, the insulin dose before the meal should be reduced, according to the type of exercise, its duration, its intensity, the training involved and above all, the person's **experience**.

The following table provides an example of how to decrease the insulin dose before the meal:

Intensity of effort	Percentage (%) reduction in the rapid or short acting insulin dose, according to duration of exercise	
	30 minutes	60 minutes
Low	25%	50%
Moderate	50%	75%
Elevated	75%	90% to 100%

Let us take, for example, a man with diabetes who injects 10 units of insulin before a meal. He plans on taking an hour-long walk at moderate intensity immediately after the meal. He can reduce the insulin dose by 75% and inject 2.5 (or 3) units before the meal.

75% x 10 units = 7.5 units

10 units – 7.5 units = 2.5 (or 3) units.

2) When the activity is **unplanned and takes place immediately before or after a meal,** or when the activity is **planned but takes place more than two hours after a meal:**
   - o **for blood glucose below 5.0 mmol/L,** have a carbohydrate snack (15 g to 30 g) at the beginning of the activity, and approximately every 30 to 45 minutes afterward, while the activity lasts;
   - o **for blood glucose above 5.0 mmol/L,** have a snack of about 15 g of carbohydrates every 30 to 45 minutes while the activity lasts.

Blood glucose should always be measured immediately **after exercising** to adjust the amounts of insulin and carbohydrates required.

In all cases, the need for insulin can decrease after exercise. This sometimes requires reducing the insulin dose for the next meal or at bedtime.

12. What can people with diabetes do to prevent hypoglycemia when exercising if they are taking oral antidiabetic drugs that stimulate the secretion of insulin?

For people with diabetes who are taking **drugs that stimulate the pancreas to produce insulin (for example, glyburide, gliclazide, repaglinide)**, the only way to lower the risk of hypoglycemia is to consume more carbohydrates while exercising. Anyone who regularly experiences hypoglycemia after exercising, however, is strongly advised to contact his or her doctor.

The recommendations are:
   - o **for blood glucose below 5.0 mmol/L,** have a carbohydrate snack (15 g to 30 g) at the beginning of the activity and then approximately every 30 to 45 minutes afterwards, while the activity lasts.

    o   **for blood glucose above 5.0 mmol/L**, additional carbohydrates are only necessary if the hypoglycemia occurs during the exercise. It is essential to check the blood glucose levels before eating, in order to avoid overeating. If more carbohydrates are needed, have a snack of about 15 g of carbohydrates every 30 to 45 minutes during the activity can provide what is necessary.

The following chart* can serve as a guide for adding carbohydrates during exercise. Additional carbohydrates are especially useful during unplanned exercise and almost always necessary during exercise that lasts a long time or is quite intense, resulting in a significant expenditure of energy.

Type of exercise	Blood glucose (mmol/L)	Additional carbohydrates
Short duration (< 30 min) at light intensity	< 5.0 > 5.0	10 g to 15 g not necessary
Moderate duration (30 to 60 min) at moderate intensity	< 5.0 5.0 - 9.9 10.0 - 13.9	30 g to 45 g 15 g every 30 to 45 min of exercise not necessary
Long duration (> 60 min) at elevated intensity	< 5.0 5.0 - 9.9 > 9.9	45 g 30 g to 45 g 15 g per hour

*Adapted from Hayes C. *J Am Diet Assoc 97* (suppl 2): S167-S171

13. What precautions are appropriate for people with diabetes who take insulin or oral antidiabetic drugs that stimulate the secretion of insulin?

People with diabetes treated with insulin or oral antidiabetic drugs that stimulate the secretion of insulin must do the following:

1) always measure blood glucose before, during and after a session of exercise, and more often than normal in the 24 hours following prolonged physical activity;
2) always carry foods containing carbohydrates to correct hypoglycemia.

14. Should exercise be done in one long session or several shorter ones?

A 30-minute session of exercise has a hypoglycemic effect, which is often desired, but it also requires adjusting insulin doses or eating more carbohydrates. The same amount of exercise performed in three ten-minute sessions has little hypoglycemic effect and requires little or no insulin adjustment or additional carbohydrates, but it still provides the sought-after benefits.

Risk of hypoglycemia from physical activity according to antidiabetic medication*	
Class of medication	**Risk of hypoglycemia**
Biguanides (e.g., metformin)	No
Alpha-glucosidase inhibitors (e.g., acarbose)	No
DPP-4 inhibitors (e.g., sitagliptin)	No
Thiazolidinedione (e.g., pioglitazone)	No
Sulfonylureas (p. ex., glyburide)	Yes
Non-sulfonylurea secretagogues (e.g., repaglinide)	Yes
Insulin	Yes

* People taking drugs associated with a risk of hypoglycemia must speak with their doctor about dose adjustment or whether to ingest carbohydrates when exercising.

Hyperglycemic Emergencies:
Diabetic Acidosis and the
Hyperosmolar State

1.   **What are the two hyperglycemic emergencies that can affect a person with diabetes?**
     The two hyperglycemic emergencies that can affect a person with diabetes are:
     - o   diabetic acidosis;
     - o   the hyperosmolar state.

     These two conditions are caused by a lack of insulin. Diabetic acidosis is more common in people with type 1 diabetes. Hyperosmolar states occur primarily in people with type 2 diabetes, usually when they are older. It is possible, however, for both conditions to occur simultaneously in people with either type 1 or type 2 diabetes.

2.   **What is diabetic acidosis?**
     Diabetic acidosis is caused by a lack of insulin. It is characterized by hyperglycemia and an accumulation of ketone bodies in the blood. The ketone bodies, which are acids, are produced by the breakdown of fats. They make the blood acidic, which can cause **excessive fatigue, abdominal pains, nausea and vomiting**. Diabetic acidosis also gives the breath a fruity odour and causes intense thirst as well as deep and rapid breathing; in some cases, it provokes disorientation and confusion. It can also sometimes result in a **coma**, which can be fatal if not treated.

Diabetic acidosis occurs primarily in people with type 1 diabetes, although it can also occur in people with type 2 diabetes when there are other aggravating factors such as infection, myocardial infarction (heart attack), pancreatitis or stroke.

3. What causes diabetic acidosis?

Diabetic acidosis is always caused by a **shortage of insulin** in the blood. When there is insufficient insulin, glucose cannot enter certain cells of the body and accumulates in the blood at extremely high levels. The body is then forced to draw on its reserves of fat for energy. The **breakdown of fats** causes the liver to produce ketone bodies. The ketone bodies, which are acids, then accumulate in the blood and spill over into the urine.

This complication of diabetes can occur if **insulin injections are skipped or doses miscalculated.**

Diabetic acidosis is sometimes caused by an **increased need for insulin** (this can happen, for example, when a person gets an infection or is under exceptional stress).

4. How is diabetic acidosis detected?

Diabetic acidosis is detected by the **presence of ketone bodies** in the urine or blood; these are accompanied by elevated blood glucose levels, often higher than **20 mmol/L**.

5. How can diabetic acidosis be avoided?

Diabetic acidosis can be avoided in most cases by taking the following precautions:
1) **Check blood glucose levels regularly.** If necessary, check for ketone bodies in the urine using Ketostix® test strips or determine the level of ketone bodies in a blood sample from the fingertip, using the Precision Xtra® meter. Take these readings **more frequently** when ill, under exceptional stress, and especially if glucose readings are **higher than 14 mmol/L**.
2) Follow a **dietician-recommended meal plan.**
3) **Take insulin** as prescribed.

4) **Follow the advice and instructions** of the doctor and dietician concerning the nutrients that should be ingested in both solid and liquid form and the **insulin** doses that should be injected when an illness makes it difficult or impossible to follow a normal diet.

5) **Call the doctor or go to the emergency room if any one of the following five situations occurs:**
   o **blood glucose is higher than 20 mmol/L;**
   o the **ketosis level reading (ketone bodies) in the urine is moderate (4 mmol/L) or large (8 mmol/L –16 mmol/L);**
   o **the ketosis level reading from the fingertip is above 3 mmol/L;**
   o **you are vomiting continually and cannot retain liquids;**
   o the **following conditions persist** despite treatment: excessive fatigue, weakness, dizziness, abdominal pains, nausea and vomiting, fruity breath odour, intense thirst, fast and heavy breathing.

6.   What is a hyperosmolar state?

A hyperosmolar state usually occurs in people with type 2 diabetes who develop an **increased resistance to insulin**. Insulin resistance prevents **glucose** from entering the cells properly, leading to its **accumulation in the blood.**

If kidney function is slightly impaired, it is more difficult to eliminate excess sugar in the blood through the urine. Sugar can therefore accumulate in the blood until it reaches very high levels (**above 30 mmol/L**), especially if not enough fluids are ingested. The small amount of insulin present in the blood at this point is usually sufficient to prevent the breakdown of fats, however, and diabetic acidosis generally does not develop.

In a hyperosmolar state, blood glucose levels rise and the person feels extremely tired and thirsty (although some elderly people feel no thirst). Frequent and profuse urination also occurs, leading to dehydration. This can be followed by a drop in blood pressure and in some cases disorientation, which can lead to coma and, if left untreated, even death.

7. What causes a hyperosmolar state?

In all cases, a hyperosmolar state is caused by a **shortage of insulin** in the blood. Because there is not a complete absence of insulin, however, ketone bodies do not form and diabetic acidosis does not develop.

This complication of diabetes can occur if antidiabetic drugs (insulin or pills) are **skipped**.

A hyperosmolar state is sometimes caused by an **increased need for insulin** (for example, in the case of illness, infection or exceptional stress, or when the subject is using certain medications such as cortisone).

Most of the time, a hyperosmolar state occurs in people who **do not feel thirst** or who are unable to hydrate themselves, which is sometimes the case for elderly people or individuals who have lost autonomy.

8. How is a hyperosmolar state detected?

The symptoms of a hyperosmolar state are generally **intense thirst, frequent and increased urination over several days**, and in particular, **blood glucose levels over 30 mmol/L**. There is usually no accumulation of ketone bodies in the blood or urine.

9. How can a hyperosmolar state be avoided?

The following tips can generally help a person avoid a hyperosmolar state.

1) **Stay hydrated**; drink 250 mL of water every hour if blood glucose levels are high or if high glucose levels cause an increased amount and frequency of urination.
2) **Measure blood glucose levels regularly** during illness or in times of exceptional stress.
3) **Follow the meal plan** recommended by the dietician.
4) Take antidiabetic **drugs** (pills or insulin) as prescribed.
5) **Follow the recommendations** of the doctor and dietician concerning the appropriate **nutrients** to consume in solid and liquid form and the **antidiabetic drug dosages** (pills or insulin) to be taken when illness makes it impossible to follow a normal diet.

Suggested approach to the detection and treatment of diabetic acidosis and/or hyperosmolar states			
Blood glucose (mmol/L)	**Ketosis level reading (mmol/L) in urine or blood**	**Symptoms**	**Suggested action**
13 - 14	None, or trace Urine: 0.5 Blood: less than 0.6	Frequent urination Intense thirst	• Drink 250 ml of water every hour • Measure blood glucose levels every 6 hours
14 - 20	Small Urine: 1.5 Blood: 0.6 to 1.5	Frequent urination Intense thirst	• Drink 250 ml of water every hour • Measure blood glucose every 4 hours • Adjust insuline doses according to the **rules of adjustment** • Contact your doctor
14 - 20	Moderate Urine: 4 Blood: 1.5 to 3	Frequent urination Intense thirst Nausea Vomiting Abdominal pain (Diarrhea)	• Measure blood glucose and ketone bodies every 4 hours • **Immediately** adjust the insulin dose to follow the **sick day recommendations** (see boxed insert, next page) • Contact the doctor or go to the emergency room if there is no improvement
More than 20	Moderate to large Urine: 8 to 13 Blood: more than 3	Nausea Vomiting Abdominal pain (Diarrhea) Fruity breath	• Go to the hospital*
More than 30	None or small Urine: 0 to 1.5 Blood: 0 to 0.6	Frequent urination Intense thirst Extreme weakness	• Go to the hospital**

*   Diabetic acidosis
** Hyperosmolar state

SLIDING SCALE FOR ADJUSTING INSULIN DOSES ON SICK DAYS

For example, in addition to units calculated for meals, one unit of rapid- or short-acting insulin may be added for each mmol/L above a blood glucose level of 14 mmol/L before each meal, at bedtime or if necessary, at night.

Example : **Lunch:** Carbohydrate content of meal = 60 g
Ratio = 1.0 unit/10 g of carbohydrates
Blood glucose = 23 mmol/L
Ketone bodies = moderate
If measured in the urine: 4 mmol/L
If measured in the blood: 1.5 to 3 mmol/L

Inject:
1) **Meal:**

$$\frac{1.0 \text{ unit } \times 60 \text{ g}}{10 \text{ g}} = 6 \text{ units}$$

2) **Adjustment of insulin doses for sick days:**
23 mmol/L − 14 mmol/L = 9 units for dosage adjustment

3) **total amount to inject:**
6 units for the meal + 9 units for dosage adjustment = 15 units

SUMMARY

Appropriate action is determined on the basis of:

1) blood sugar levels;
2) the presence or absence of ketone bodies in the blood or urine;
3) the presence of signs and symptoms.

Chronic Complications

1. What are the long-term complications of diabetes?

After several years, if blood glucose levels are not well managed, complications can develop and affect:
1) the **eyes (diabetic retinopathy)**;
2) the **kidneys (diabetic nephropathy)**;
3) the **nervous system (diabetic neuropathy)**;
4) the **heart** and **blood vessels (cardiac or peripheral atherosclerosis)**.

2. How does diabetes affect the eyes?

Over time, hyperglycemia can cause **changes to the small vessels in the back of the eye** that can compromise blood circulation and cause hemorrhage: this is called **diabetic retinopathy.** If diabetes and retinopathy are not adequately treated, they can lead to blindness. Diabetic retinopathy is the leading cause of blindness in the 20 to 64 year old age group.

3. How do I know if my eyes have been affected by diabetes?

If your eyes are affected, you may see **spiderwebs** or **spots** in your field of vision. Consult an ophthalmologist (a doctor who specializes in eye diseases) or an optometrist, who will examine the eyes by dilating the pupil to take a look at the retina. Examinations with special digital cameras that take photos of the back of the eye can also detect abnormalities. If any are found, an examination by an ophthalmologist is necessary to confirm the diagnosis. Temporary changes in vision (blurriness) can result from blood glucose variations. **Hyperglycemia and hypoglycemia can cause blurry vision**, which is corrected when blood glucose is normalized.

4. When should I have my eyes examined?

It is fairly common for damage to the retina, a light sensitive layer at the back of the eye, to occur without causing any vision problems. It is therefore very **important to consult an ophthalmologist or optometrist regularly.**

People with type 1 diabetes should consult an ophthalmologist or optometrist five years after the initial diagnosis and once a year afterwards. People with type 2 diabetes should consult an ophthalmologist or optometrist at the time of diagnosis and every one to two years afterwards. In the case of both type 1 and type 2 diabetes, however, it might be necessary to visit an ophthalmologist more often if the eyes show any signs of damage progression.

5. How can I protect my eyes?

The eyes can be protected by:
1) keeping **blood glucose levels** as close to normal as possible;
2) consulting an **ophthalmologist** or **optometrist** regularly;
3) controlling your **blood pressure**;
4) **quitting smoking**, if applicable.

6. What are the possible long-term of diabetes on the kidneys?

In the long term, hyperglycemia can cause changes in the **small blood vessels of the kidneys**, compromising their blood filtration and purification functions: this is called **diabetic nephropathy**. If diabetes is not properly controlled, this condition can develop into complete loss of renal function. In such a case, dialysis (artificial kidney) or a kidney transplant is necessary. Diabetes is the main cause of dialysis in the Western world.

7. How do I know if my kidneys have been affected by diabetes?

The effect of diabetes on the kidneys can only be detected through a laboratory analysis to detect **microalbuminuria** (small amounts of albumin in the urine). This test requires only a urine sample. In some cases, the doctor will ask for urine samples from a 24 hour period to better assess the severity of the nephropathy. A rise in blood pressure can also signal the onset of damage to the kidneys.

8. How can I protect my kidneys?

The kidneys can be protected by:
1) keeping **blood glucose levels** as close to normal as possible;
2) checking for **albumin** in the urine once a year;
3) checking **blood pressure** regularly and treating high blood pressure aggressively;
4) **quitting smoking**, if applicable;
5) taking drugs to slow the progression of the nephropathy. These drugs are also used to control blood pressure and heart failure. The doctor may suggest them if indicated.

9. What are the possible long-term effects of diabetes on the nerves?

In the long term, hyperglycemia can **damage the nerves**, particularly in the extremities but also in such organs as the intestines, stomach, bladder, heart and genitals. This is known as **diabetic neuropathy**.

10. How do I know if the nerves in my extremities have been affected by diabetes?

In most cases, nerve damage manifests as a **decrease in sensitivity of the extremities to pain, heat and cold**. Another sign is a tingling or burning sensation. The diagnosis can be confirmed by your doctor or by a special test called electromyography (EMG). This type of complication is also known as "peripheral diabetic neuropathy" and affects the lower limbs more often than the upper limbs.

11. What is the biggest danger when nerves in the extremities are affected?

The biggest danger of a loss of sensation, particularly in the feet, is **unwilling self-injury** (from ill-fitting shoes, hot water, a needle, etc.). After such an injury, infection can occur and, if circulation is compromised, can lead to gangrene and amputation.

12. How do I know if the nerves in my intestines have been affected by diabetes?

When the nerves in the intestines are affected by diabetes, stool evacuation can be compromised: this is called **constipation**. In an advanced state, when stools stagnate in the colon, normal intestinal bacteria can multiply, liquefying the stool and triggering sudden, intense diarrhea several times a day, especially at night: this is called **diabetic diarrhea.**

The first line of treatment for constipation is diet. Fibre consumption should be increased gradually and plenty of water consumed. Fibre supplements in capsules or powder form (e.g. Metamucil®) can help make the stool firmer and help with evacuation. If fibre and water are not effective, there are drugs available to treat constipation.

Constipation can be treated with drugs that cause the intestines to contract (for example, domperidone or metoclopramide). Laxatives, such as docusate sodium or sennosides, are also an option.

Diabetic diarrhea can also be treated with antibiotics such as tetracycline or erythromycin. Sometimes, anti-diarrheal agents such as loperamide or diphenoxylate must be added.

13. How do I know if the nerves of my stomach have been affected by diabetes?

When the nerves of the stomach are affected, the stomach empties more slowly: this is **diabetic gastroparesis.** This usually manifests as a feeling of bloating and/or regurgitation after a meal. Food absorption becomes irregular, which can explain poor control of blood glucose (hyperglycemia and hypoglycemia). The diagnosis can be confirmed by a nuclear medicine test called gastric emptying.

Gastroparesis can be treated with small and frequent meals and, if necessary, drugs such as domperidone or metoclopramide that cause the stomach to contract. In very serious cases, a gastric pacemaker can sometimes improve the symptoms.

14. How do I know if the nerves of my bladder have been affected by diabetes?

When the nerves of the bladder are affected by diabetes, it is more difficult to sense when the bladder is full. Furthermore, the bladder does not empty completely during urination: this is called **neurogenic bladder**. It can result in overflow loss of urine and, if urine stagnates in the bladder, there is a risk of urinary tract infection that can extend to the kidneys.

Neurogenic bladder can be diagnosed with an echography of the bladder after urination, which will reveal any urine retention.

To avoid overflow loss of urine, it is advised to urinate regularly, while exerting pressure on the bladder. In the case of significant urine retention, drugs that cause the bladder to contract such as betanechol can be used.

Nerve damage to the bladder can also manifest as hyperactive bladder, which has the following symptoms:
- increased frequency of urination;
- urgency of urination;
- urinary incontinence.

This condition results from damage to the nerves, causing them to send a signal to the bladder to contract at inappropriate times. Drugs such as oxybutinine (Ditropan®, Oxytrol®) can help control these symptoms.

15. How do I know if the nerves of my heart have been affected by diabetes?

Most of the time, when the nerves of the heart are affected, the condition is asymptomatic. In some cases, an accelerated heartbeat (tachycardia) and/or arrhythmia are noticeable. The diagnosis can be confirmed by electrocardiogram (ECG).

There is no specific treatment. If the accelerated heartbeat persists, beta-blockers such as metoprolol, atenolol, etc. can be prescribed.

16. How does a man know if the nerves in his genitals have been affected by diabetes?

When the nerves in the genitals are affected, men with diabetes have difficulty achieving and maintaining erection, making sexual relations difficult or impossible; this is known as **erectile dysfunction**.

This can be treated with certain oral medications such as Viagra®, Cialis® and Levitra®. Sometimes, more aggressive treatments are necessary, such as prostaglandin, either introduced into the urethra (urinary duct) in the form of suppositories (for example, Muse®) or injected into the base of the penis (for example, Caverject®).

17. How can nerve problems and their complications be prevented?

Nerve problems and their complications can be prevented by:
1) keeping **blood glucose levels** as close to normal as possible;
2) taking measures to avoid **trauma** and **burns** to the feet;
3) **inspecting the feet** daily;
4) consulting a **doctor** in the event of even the slightest lesion;
5) reporting any **digestive problems**;
6) reporting any **bladder problems**;
7) reporting any **erectile dysfunction**;
8) reporting any **accelerated or irregular heartbeat**;
9) seeking aggressive treatment for **high blood pressure**.

18. How can diabetes affect the heart and blood vessels?

Diabetes can affect the heart and blood vessels by accelerating the process of **arteriosclerosis**. This is a thickening and hardening of the arteries, which can block circulation in certain parts of the body, such as the heart, lower limbs, and even the brain. Damage to the blood vessels in the heart is the main cause of morbidity and death in people with diabetes.

19. What are the possible dangers of damage to the heart and blood vessels?

The dangers of arteriosclerosis depend on the part of the body affected:
1) if the heart is affected, **myocardial infarction** can result;
2) if the brain is affected, a **stroke can result, possibly causing paralysis or speech impairment**;
3) if the lower limbs are affected, **pain when walking** and **intermittent claudication can result**.

20. How do I know if my heart and blood vessels have been affected by diabetes?

Certain signs reveal arteriosclerosis and circulation problems:
1) **slow healing** of wounds;
2) **chest pain** and/or **difficulty breathing** during physical exertion;
3) **pain in the calves** when walking (intermittent claudication).

In some cases, however, arteriosclerosis is asymptomatic, particularly in its early stages, and can be diagnosed only by medical examination or by means of special tests such as an electrocardiogram at rest or during exertion, cardiac scintigraphy (MIBI), abdominal X-ray (to identify vessel calcification), or a Doppler test (to examine the condition of blood vessels using ultrasound) of vessels in the neck or the lower limbs.

21. How can I prevent damage to my heart and blood vessels due to my diabetes?

Reduce the risk of damage to the heart and blood vessels by:
1) keeping **blood glucose levels** as close to normal as possible;
2) checking **blood pressure** regularly and treating high blood pressure aggressively;
3) avoiding **saturated fats** (especially of animal origin) as much as possible;
4) having **blood lipid levels** checked regularly and treating any anomalies aggressively;
5) **quitting smoking**, if applicable;
6) **exercising**;
7) taking an **aspirin a day** (unless contraindicated).

22. What is high blood pressure?

In the general population, blood pressure is considered high if it is greater than or equal to 140/90. In people with diabetes, however, the criteria are more rigorous and blood pressure is considered high if it is greater than or equal to 130/80.

23. Why should people with diabetes treat high blood pressure aggressively?

High blood pressure significantly increases the complications of diabetes that affect the eyes, nerves, kidneys, heart and blood vessels.

It has been clearly shown that treating high blood pressure in people with diabetes significantly decreases the development and progression of complications associated with the disease.

24. What is considered a blood lipid anomaly in a person with diabetes?

A person with diabetes is said to have a blood lipid anomaly if:
1) bad cholesterol (LDL cholesterol) is greater than 2 mmol/L;
2) good cholesterol (HDL cholesterol) is less than 1.0 mmol/L;
3) triglycerides are greater than or equal to 1.5 mmol/L; or
4) the ratio between total cholesterol and HDL cholesterol is greater than or equal to 4.0.

25. Why should all blood lipid anomalies be treated aggressively?

Blood lipid anomalies should be treated aggressively because they represent major risk factors for arteriosclerosis and therefore for diseases of the heart and blood vessels. Because people with diabetes have an elevated risk of developing diseases of the heart and blood vessels, these anomalies must be treated with added vigilance.

Foot Care and General Hygiene

1. **Why is diabetic foot a public health issue?**

    Foot complications due to diabetes are a major public health issue because they are the primary cause of non-trauma-related amputations. In the long term, poorly controlled diabetes is associated with peripheral neuropathy, especially of the feet. Loss of sensitivity to touch, pain, heat and cold are some of the symptoms. This loss of sensitivity makes people with diabetes vulnerable to injuries that go unnoticed. A lesion can become infected and if there are circulatory problems, gangrene can develop, possibly requiring amputation. However, if people with diabetes take good care of their feet, 80% of these amputations can be prevented. Hence the importance of learning about proper foot care.

2. **What problems can lead to diabetic foot complications in people with diabetes?**

    The feet of people with diabetes are more fragile than those of people who do not have the disease. In the long term, hyperglycemia can cause the following foot problems:
    1) **nerve damage** resulting in loss of sensitivity to touch, pain, heat and cold;
    2) **a tendency for the skin to get thinner and drier**, to become more easily irritated and to develop calluses (hyperkeratosis) at pressure points;
    3) a tendency for **arteries to thicken and harden**, thereby reducing circulation in the feet;

4) **a susceptibility to infection** because the body is less able to defend itself against microbes when blood glucose levels are high.

3. How should the feet be examined?

The responsibility for foot care should be shared between the person with diabetes and his or her healthcare team. If you have diabetes, do the following to prevent complications:

1) examine your feet closely every day after a bath or shower;
2) sit down and, under a good light source, examine both feet from every angle (top, bottom and between the toes);
3) use a mirror to examine the soles of the feet if you lack the flexibility to see them otherwise;
4) ask another person for help if your vision is impaired or if you cannot reach your feet with your hands;
5) follow up the self-exam with a thorough professional examination every time you visit a doctor, podiatrist or nurse specializing in foot care.

4. What should I look for?

Look carefully for:

1) **lesions between the toes** caused by fungi that thrive in humid conditions (athlete's foot);
2) **calluses:** heavily callused skin (often located under the foot) can make the skin fragile and vulnerable to infection, thus providing a good place for microbes to multiply;
3) **corns:**
   o   on the toes, produced by friction with shoes;
   o   between the toes, known as "soft corns" (or "kissing corns"), caused by the toes being compressed together;
4) **cracks:** crevices in callused skin (often on or around the heel) are particularly well-suited for microbial growth. Excess callused skin can always be traced to a specific cause:
   o   poor foot posture (position, compression); see your doctor as soon as possible;

o   the use of instruments that can harm the feet: razor blades, knives, graters or corn-removal preparations;

o   foreign bodies in the shoes or seams that can injure the feet; check by running your hand along the inside of your shoes.

5.   What are the first signs of foot problems?

The feet should be examined for the following problems:

1) changes in skin colour, unusual redness;
2) unusually high skin temperature;
3) swollen feet or ankles;
4) pain in the legs or feet;
5) ingrown toenails;
6) toenail fungi;
7) open sores that heal slowly;
8) calluses that bleed or appear to be infected;
9) dry and fissured skin, especially around the heel;
10) scratches;
11) bunions;
12) warts;
13) loss of sensation in the feet.

6.   How can a person with diabetes reduce the risk of foot problems?

To limit the risk of developing foot problems:

1) keep blood glucose as close to normal as possible;
2) quit smoking, if applicable;
3) lose weight, if necessary;
4) reduce alcohol consumption, if applicable;
5) get regular exercise;
6) see a doctor, podiatrist, or nurse specialized in foot care, or any other specialist, as needed.

7. What are the top-ten foot care suggestions for people with diabetes?

1) **Examine your feet every day** and ask for help from family and friends if needed:
   - examine the feet closely all over, looking for lesions, cuts or any malformation;
   - regularly check the sensitivity level of the feet (following the doctor's recommendations):
     - run a cotton ball lightly over and under the foot to detect any areas lacking sensation;
     - put a dry pea in your shoe and walk a few steps to see whether you can detect the foreign body; remove the pea immediately to avoid injuring yourself.

2) **Do not walk barefoot**, not even in the house, and especially not on a beach or in any public area:
   - put on slippers when you get out of bed;
   - during the day, wear comfortable shoes.

3) **Wash your feet every day:**
   - check the water temperature with your wrist, elbow or a thermometer; the water should be lukewarm (below 37°C);
   - wash your feet with mild soap (for example, unscented Dove®, Aveeno®, Cetaphil®, Neutrogena®, Keri®, etc.);
   - avoid soaking your feet for longer than 10 minutes to avoid maceration and softening of the skin;
   - dry your feet carefully, especially between and under the toes; humidity encourages the development of fungi such as athlete's foot.

4) **Be sure the skin is completely dry:**
   - apply a thin layer of neutral (unscented) moisturizing cream (for example, Nivea®, Lubriderm®, Vaseline Intensive Care® lotion, Glycerodermine®, etc.), except between the toes;
   - once or twice a week after a bath or shower, use a moistened pumice stone to rub areas where hyperkeratosis (thickening of the skin) has developed. Avoid rubbing back and forth, and use long, continuous movements instead. Never use a metal grater, which can cause injury.

5) **Avoid cutting your toenails too short:**
   - nails should be cut straight across, a little beyond the tips of the toes, and the corners filed after a bath or shower. This will prevent the development of ingrown toenails and wounds;

- nails should be filed with an emery board instead of being cut; this will help avoid injury;
- handle round-ended scissors and nail clippers with care. Anyone lacking in dexterity or suffering from impaired or reduced vision should avoid using them altogether;
- never tear your toenails.

6) **Never self-treat for calluses, corns or blisters:**
   - avoid so-called "bathroom surgery": never use pointy scissors, sharp clippers, razor blades, lancets, scalpels, or metal files to remove a corn;
   - never use over-the-counter solutions or plasters with a salicylic acid base; they can cause skin necrosis;
   - see a professional specializing in foot care, taking care to tell him or her that you have diabetes.

7) **Change socks every day:**
   - wear clean socks (or stockings); wash them every day;
   - wear socks that fit; be sure they are loose and long enough and do not squeeze the toes; avoid wearing tight socks that leave marks on the calves and cut off circulation;
   - avoid thick stitching; if the socks have seams, wear them inside out;
   - avoid shoes with holes or patches that create points of friction;
   - wear socks that keep the feet dry, made from a blend of cotton and synthetic fibres (acrylic, orlon, polypropylene, Coolmax, etc.); people who sweat profusely should avoid socks that contain nylon.

8) **Choose your shoes carefully:**
   - always wear socks with shoes;
   - choose shoes fastened with laces, buckles or velcro; they should be made from supple leather or canvas and roomy enough to let the toes move;
   - choose non-skid soles;
   - buy shoes in the late afternoon; when feet are swollen, it is easier to choose shoes that fit correctly;
   - break in new shoes gradually by wearing them only a half-hour a day at first;
   - carefully inspect the inside of your shoes before wearing them; run your hand inside to find any foreign bodies or seams that could injure your feet;
   - avoid pointy shoes and shoes with high heels (over 3 cm).

9) **Watch out for burns or frostbite:**
   - wear socks, even in bed, if your feet are cold; avoid hot-water bottles, electric blankets or hot water;

      o   use sunscreen with at least 15 SPF (sun protection factor) to lower the risk of sunburns;

      o   never use powerful products or irritants (for example, Parisienne® or other bleaches);

      o   make sure the skin is covered, especially in cold and dry winter weather.

10) **Immediately contact your foot care specialist** (doctor, podiatrist or nurse) if you notice discoloration, loss of sensation or a lesion.

Everyone with diabetes should have a foot examination at least twice a year. People at higher risk should have more frequent exams.

8. Which moisturizing creams should a person with diabetes use for foot care?

For skin that has a tendency to dry out, use a moisturizer daily. Unscented products without coloring are preferable. Avoid applying cream between the toes, which will soften the skin excessively. Apply a thin layer after a bath or shower.

There are three main kinds of moisturizing products:
1) **hydrating products with humectants**, which soften the skin and diminish fine lines (e.g., Nivea®, Glycerodermine®, Glaxal Base®, Aquatain®, Complex-15®, etc.);
2) **anti-dehydration products**, which reduce the evaporation of moisture by creating a film on the skin (e.g., Moisturel®, Lubriderm® (Lotion), Cetaphil®, Aveeno® (Lotion), Keri® (Lotion), Vaseline Intensive Care® (Lotion), Neutrogena®, Aquaphor®, Prevex®, Barrier Creme®, Akildia®, Curel®, Eucrin®, Elta®, etc.);
3) **hydrating products with keratolytic and exfoliating properties**, which help remove dead skin cells. These products should be **used with care and be applied only on the stratum corneum, or top layer, of the skin.** Urea may cause a burning or tingling sensation on dry or cracked skin (e.g., Uremol-10®, Uremol-20®, Dermal Therapy® at 10%, 15%, 20% or 25% urea, Lacticare® Lotion, Lac-Hydrin® Lotion, Urisec®, etc.).

9. **Which antiseptic products should a person with diabetes use for sores or lesions on the feet?**

Wash the sore with water and mild soap, then rinse and dry it well.

1) Disinfect the skin with an antiseptic (according to a doctor's recommendations):
   - 70% alcohol swab;
   - Proviodine swab;
   - 0.05% chlorhexidine gluconate (e.g., Hibidil®, Baxedin®).

2) **If there is inflammation**, apply a compress soaked in physiological saline solution three or four times a day. Watch for signs of infection over the next 24 to 48 hours. Avoid using adhesive tape directly on the skin. If redness worsens or if there is pus, see a doctor immediately.

3) **If your doctor recommends foot baths**, use one of the following products in one litre of lukewarm boiled water for no more than 10 minutes:
   - 15 ml (1 tbsp.) of Proviodine®;
   - 15 ml (1 tbsp.) of Hibitane® 4% (chlorhexidine gluconate 4%);
   - 30 ml (2 tbsp.) of Hibitane® 2% (chlorhexidine gluconate 2%).

Wash your feet again in running water and dry them well, especially between the toes. See a doctor if the sore does not heal.

It is important to discover the cause of the problem so that it is does not recur.

10. **How can circulation in the feet be improved?**

There are a number of simple, readily available methods that can improve circulation and maintain or improve the flexibility of the feet.
   - Do not smoke.
   - Do not cross your legs when sitting.
   - Keep moving – do not remain standing or sitting in one place for too long.
   - Walk as much as you can, within your limits and abilities.
   - When seated, rest your legs on a footstool whenever possible.
   - Do foot exercises regularly – repeat each one 20 times:
     - put a towel on the floor and try to pick it up with your toes;
     - stand on the tips of your toes, then lower your body weight down onto your heels; use a support if necessary (be careful not to fall);
     - flex your ankle, pointing your feet up and down;

- rotate your feet, first in one direction, then the other;
- rock in an armchair, pushing with your toes.

11. What is diabetic neuropathic pain?

The term "diabetic neuropathy" refers to nerve disease associated with diabetes. Neuropathic pain occurs when damage to the nerves causes pain.

12. What are the symptoms of diabetic neuropathic pain?

Some people with diabetes suffering from neuropathic pain use many different terms to describe it. Neuropathic pain may be accompanied by:

- o burning sensations;
- o numbness;
- o stinging;
- o tingling;
- o a feeling of electric shock;
- o sensitivity to touch or cold;
- o formication;
- o a feeling of being crushed;
- o deep, shooting pains;
- o a feeling of walking on cotton batten.

13. How is diabetic neuropathic pain treated?

People with diabetes can lower the risk of developing neuropathic complications by properly managing their blood sugar levels. In some cases, proper control of diabetes, physical exercise, meal plans and relaxation exercises combined with drug treatment can help reduce pain. The doctor may prescribe medications such as amitriptyline, gabapentine (Neurontin®) or pregabaline (Lyrica®).

14. What is a diabetic foot ulcer?

A diabetic foot ulcer is a foot sore or wound resulting from neuropathy; it develops on pressure points on the bottom of the foot, due to calluses or other foot deformations. In many cases people with diabetes continue to walk around despite such foot injuries because they lack sensitivity in their feet, unwittingly making them worse. In some cases, a sore develops in the middle of a callus, which can worsen and become infected, especially if blood glucose is poorly controlled. If the ulcer does not receive adequate treatment, it can become gangrenous and amputation may be necessary.

If you have any questions about the nature of a sore on your foot, see your doctor as quickly as possible. Foot ulcers will heal with the appropriate treatment.

15. Why is dental hygiene particularly important for people with diabetes?

People with diabetes should manage their dental health with as much care as their skin or feet for two major reasons:

1) Poorly controlled diabetes causes a high risk of cavities, gum sores or infection.
2) Any infection can raise blood glucose levels and hamper the control of diabetes.

16. What are the main types of oral lesions?

1) **Cavities**

   Cavities destroy teeth. The main cause of cavities is dental plaque, a whitish deposit that sticks to the enamel. The formation of dental plaque is encouraged by sweet foods, failure to brush the teeth and gums, and alcohol, which reduces acidity levels in the mouth.

2) **Gingivitis**

   Gingivitis is caused by the deposit of bacteria that create plaque between the teeth and gums. The gum becomes bright red, inflamed and swollen, and tends to bleed if touched.

3) **Periodontitis**

   Periodontitis develops if gingivitis remains untreated. The germs along the roots of the affected teeth multiply, and the inflammation spreads to areas deep within the gums and the bone supporting the teeth. The teeth become loose and may even fall out painlessly.

17. What kind of dental hygiene measures should people with diabetes practice?

The main preventive dental hygiene measures are:

1) maintain blood glucose levels as close to normal as possible;
2) brush your teeth carefully after every meal;
3) use dental floss every day;
4) see a dentist twice a year or more often if necessary;
5) see a denturologist once every five years to adjust dental prostheses, if necessary;
6) consume alcohol in moderation, so as not to reduce acidity in the mouth;
7) do not smoke.

People with diabetes should always inform the health professionals they consult that they have diabetes. In the event of an intervention, antibiotics may be prescribed to prevent infection.

Living with Diabetes

1. What does it mean to live with diabetes?

Diabetes is increasingly widespread. Many people, however, find that **it is not easy to live with diabetes**.

People who have been diagnosed with diabetes face a series of challenges that will be there for the rest of their lives. These challenges include the following:
1) **Realizing that diabetes is a chronic illness** that cannot be cured.
2) **Admitting that it is a serious illness,** even if the symptoms are barely noticeable and not painful.
3) **Accepting the necessity of establishing a daily routine** (meals, sleeping, exercise, etc.), especially if insulin treatment is necessary.
4) **Self-motivating to change certain habits,** since medication alone is not enough to treat diabetes.
5) **Taking personal responsibility** for treatment.

The challenges of living with diabetes are considerable, but surmountable.

2. Is there anything to help a person who has just been diagnosed with diabetes?

Advances in knowledge about diabetes in terms of both medical science and the psychosocial sphere are cause for optimism. People with diabetes should remember the following:
1) diabetes **can be controlled effectively**;
2) good control of blood glucose **significantly decreases the risks of developing serious complications** over the long term;
3) there are information and training resources (such as diabetes teaching units) that allows people with diabetes to acquire the necessary skills to **adapt diabetes treatment to daily life and individual needs**;

4) diabetes can be an **opportunity to learn** how to improve diet, exercise regularly, manage stress more effectively, and generally learn how to live better.

Most people with diabetes are able to live long, active, healthy and satisfying lives.

3. How do people with diabetes accept their illness?

A diagnosis of diabetes delivers an emotional shock, whether or not the person is aware of it. The shock is provoked by the need to face up to the reality that the disease will inevitably entail some losses.

Whether or not the person wants to, he or she will begin a grieving process, which will eventually, at the person's own speed, lead to a state of acceptance of the illness and its treatment.

A better understanding of the disease can make the grieving process a little easier. Acceptance comes through knowledge; it is therefore important to learn about the disease.

4. What is a grieving process?

Grieving is a process of maturation that everyone goes through when they deal with a loss. In the case of diabetes, the process involves grieving the loss of health, along with other equally important losses, such as the loss of liberty, spontaneity, and former habits. It can even involve grieving the loss of self-esteem or a feeling of invulnerability.

The grieving process evolves in a number of stages that correspond to different emotions that vary in intensity and duration. These emotions, which are entirely normal, help the person with diabetes reach a new state of emotional equilibrium and greater acceptance.

5. What are the stages of grief?

The following chart presents the five stages of grief. They may appear in a different order, according to the individual.

Stage	Description	Characteristic statements
1) Denial or negation	Ignoring the unbearable aspects of the illness or treatment. Acting as though there is no illness or as though it is not serious.	"I can't be diabetic, I don't feel sick."
2) Anger or revolt	Seeing the illness as an injustice. Being angry at everyone. Blaming others. Seeing only the negative aspects of treatment.	"Diabetes is the worst disease possible, and it's preventing me from living my life."
3) Negociating or bargaining	Taking on certain aspects of the disease, but leaving out whatever is displeasing. Acceptance remains very conditional.	"I take pills to lower my blood sugar, so I don't have to worry about what I eat."
4) Depressive feelings or reflection	Realizing that denying the illness is useless. Exaggerated perception of limitations. Possible feelings of powerless or retreating into dependency.	"Is this kind of life worth living?"
5) Acceptance	Realistic perception of the illness and its treatment. Deciding to take concrete and positive action.	"I'd rather not have diabetes, but since I don't have a choice, I'm going to do my best."

6. How can the grieving process be influenced and acceptance encouraged?

Being open to actively learning about the process will make the stages of grief more clearly recognizable and make it possible to identify the related emotions. Above all, it will help the person with diabetes get in touch with himself or herself through these emotions. This is a journey of self-discovery.

The next step involves learning to transform negative feelings, whether guilt, anger or fear, into positive ones. It is normal to have negative feelings or emotions, and they are not bad in themselves. They are simply unpleasant.

Being aware of negative feelings can help motivate the will to change. They are often the expression of psychological pain related to specific problems. The best way to ease this pain is to find solutions to the problems that cause them.

These steps can influence the grieving process and thereby the process of acceptance, which ultimately makes it possible to adapt to the disease and its treatment.

7. Are some emotional problems more common in people with diabetes?

Yes. We know that depression and anxiety affect a good number of people in the general population, but studies suggest that **depression** and **anxiety disorders** are more common in people with a chronic physical illness such as diabetes.

It is estimated that depression affects people with diabetes up to three times more than those in the general population (20% compared to 5% to 10%). Similarly, anxiety disorders are up to six times more common (30% compared to 5%).

Accurate diagnosis of these two psychological problems is therefore important, since they can significantly influence the control of blood glucose. The more depressed or anxious a person feels, the harder it is to control the diabetes.

8. How is depression recognized?

It is first necessary to distinguish between depressive feelings, which are normal emotions that play a part in the grieving process, and depression, which is an illness. Someone whose mood is depressed will not necessarily be diagnosed with depression.

Depression **becomes an illness** when the symptoms listed below last several weeks and begin to **affect work and social life**:
1) feeling depressed, sad, hopeless, discouraged, "at the end of my rope" most of the day, almost every day;
2) loss of interest or pleasure in almost all activities;
3) loss of or significant increase in appetite or weight;
4) insomnia or a need to sleep more than usual;
5) agitation (for example, difficulty sitting still) or the slowing down of psychomotor

functions (for example, slowed speech, monotone voice, long delay before answering questions, slower bodily movements);

6) lack of energy, tiredness;

7) feelings of loss of dignity, self-blame, excessive or inappropriate guilt;

8) difficulty concentrating, thinking or making a decision;

9) recurring thoughts of death, suicidal impulses, death wishes or actual suicide attempts.

9. What should you do if you think you are suffering from depression?

If you have experienced some or many of these symptoms for at least two weeks, inform your doctor to determine whether the symptoms are due to diabetes, other physical problems (for example, hypothyroidism) or depression. The doctor can then prescribe the appropriate treatment or refer you to a mental health specialist, as needed.

Although depressive feelings are often a normal part of the grieving process after a diagnosis of diabetes, a doctor should be consulted if these feelings intensify and last for several weeks.

Depression is one of the most easily treated mental health problems, especially if diagnosed promptly. Most people who suffer from depression are treated with antidepressant medications and/or psychotherapy, and the combination of these two therapeutic approaches has been recognized as the most effective treatment. The support of family, friends and outreach groups is also important.

10. How are anxiety disorders recognized?

Anxiety disorders are mental health problems in which anxiety is the predominant disturbance. In people with diabetes, anxiety disorders such as phobias (for example, a fear of needles or of low blood glucose) and especially **generalized anxiety** are the most frequent.

A diagnosis of a generalized anxiety disorder is possible if the following symptoms are present:

1) anxiety and excessive worry most of the time, for at least six months, with respect to different events or activities;

2) difficulty controlling this type of worry;

3) intense distress;
4) agitation or feeling on edge;
5) easily fatigued;
6) difficulty concentrating or memory lapses;
7) irritability;
8) muscle tension;
9) disturbed sleep.

11. What should you do if you think you are suffering from an anxiety disorder?

If you show signs of generalized anxiety or a phobia, speak to your doctor, who will evaluate your situation and recommend the appropriate treatment or refer you to a mental health professional, as needed.

Anxiety disorders can be treated with drugs and/or psychotherapy. Relaxation techniques are common therapeutic tools to treat these conditions.

12. Where can you find help if you suffer from depression?

Speak to your doctor. In some cases, if indicated, drug treatment can begin right away. Your doctor can also refer you to a mental health professional, that is, a psychiatrist or psychologist who works in the public healthcare system. You can find these professionals at a hospital's department of psychiatry or psychology, or through the mental health services offered by some Community Health Centres.

Psychiatrists and psychologists in private practice are also available for consultation. Their contact information is available through their respective professional associations.

13. Is it true that people with diabetes go through personality changes and become angrier or more aggressive?

No. **Anger is not a typical personality trait of people with diabetes**. There of course may be people with diabetes who are short-tempered, but this has nothing to do with the fact that they have the disease.

However, **sudden character changes** or irritable or angry **mood swings** could be a sign that a person with diabetes is **in a hypoglycemic state**. These signs will disappear once the hypoglycemia has been corrected.

Mood swings can also occur **when a person with diabetes becomes very tired** because of elevated or fluctuating blood glucose. These mood swings usually stop relatively quickly when blood glucose is better controlled and the person recovers energy.

Irritability can also **signify a failure to accept the illness**. In such cases, the people have become "embittered by their illness". This phenomenon is not specific to diabetes and can be experienced by anyone with a chronic disease who has been unable to accept the condition.

It is therefore important for people who are near a diabetic person to be able to distinguish the different reasons for any mood swings. This will make it easier to understand and help.

Remember:

o Your personality shapes how you react to your diabetes.

o You cannot totally control the emotions you feel or even the way you manage them, but you are responsible for your behaviour.

o You cannot control the time it takes to go through the grieving process, but you are responsible for learning about it, observing your reactions, and influencing the process if possible.

o Your diabetes is not your fault, but managing it is your responsibility.

Managing Daily Stress

1. **Why should people with diabetes be concerned about daily stress?**

    Stress can increase blood glucose levels in some people with diabetes. Stress acts directly on blood glucose by encouraging the secretion of hormones such as adrenalin, which release glucose reserves from the liver into the bloodstream and decrease the effectiveness of insulin by increasing resistance to it in the cells. Stress can also act indirectly by causing people to neglect their self-care.

2. **Does stress cause diabetes?**

    No, it does not. In someone who is genetically predisposed, however, stress can be one of the factors that trigger the disease.

3. **What is stress?**

    Stress is what you feel when you think that you are unable to effectively deal with a situation that you perceive as threatening.

    The following four characteristics create a stressful situation: the feeling of a lack of control over the situation, its unpredictability, its newness, and the feeling of a threatened ego. The brain detects a stressful situation and responds to the stress only if at least one of these four characteristics is present.

    Stress is largely the result of an individual's perception of an event, and not simply the event itself.

Stress is a part of life. No one can go through life without encountering stress. Essentially, it is a coping mechanism that has enabled humanity to survive. Everyone has a different tolerance to stress and, depending on a number of factors, it can be experienced as either good or bad.

4. What is "good stress"?

A person's capacity to deal with a threatening situation effectively is what determines whether or not that person perceives stress as good or bad. It can be a positive force in a person's life. For example, resolving a very difficult problem and falling in love are events that potentially cause good stress because they increase the pleasure and satisfaction that can be taken from life. On the other hand, if these situations are perceived by the person as beyond his or her ability to deal with them, the stress will probably be experienced more intensely and perceived as bad.

5. What are the sources of stress?

Stressors fall into three broad categories:

1) **physical stressors:**
   o   illness and its consequences;
   o   fatigue;
   o   pain.

2) **psychological stressors:**
   o   emotions;
   o   attitudes;
   o   behaviour.

3) **social stressors:**
   o   interpersonal and professional relationships;
   o   death of a loved one;
   o   major life changes (marriage, moving, retirement).

It should be noted that stress can be triggered by happy events (marriage, birth of a child, promotion) as well as difficult ones.

6. What affects a person's response to stress?

Several factors affect a person's response to stress, including:

1) **personal factors**: personality, genetics, past experiences, attitudes;
2) **emotions**: guilt, anxiety, sadness, fear, etc.;
3) **personal resources**: coping strategies, social support, information.

7. How are the symptoms of stress recognized?

There are many possible indicators of stress:

1) **physical symptoms:**
    o   increased heartbeat;
    o   rise in blood pressure;
    o   increased muscle tension;
    o   faster breathing;
    o   chronic fatigue;
    o   headache, backache;
    o   tightness in the chest;
    o   digestive problems;
    o   tics, twitching.

2) **psychological symptoms:**
    o   aggressiveness;
    o   depression;
    o   crying jags or an inability to cry;
    o   feeling empty, dissatisfied;
    o   ambivalence;
    o   decreased ability to concentrate or pay attention;
    o   decreased motivation;
    o   loss of self-esteem;
    o   nightmares.

3) **behavioural symptoms:**
    o   irritability;
    o   angry outbursts;
    o   very critical attitude;
    o   forgetfulness, indecision;
    o   loss of productivity;

o   increased consumption of some foods or substances (tobacco, alcohol, medications) or loss of appetite;

o   sexual problems.

Although humans are equipped to deal adequately with occasional stress, persistent, intense and frequent stress can overtax our bodies and cause undesirable physical states. Stress is a part of human life and cannot be eliminated. It is possible, however, to learn how to manage and minimize its negative effects.

8. How should you respond to stress?

1) **Recognize your stress level**: First, know how to recognize the symptoms and sources of stress. Awareness of your own stress level is a starting point.

2) **Recognize good stress and bad stress**: Understand what makes stress positive or negative for you.

3) **Develop strategies to cope with stress**: Research on coping strategies has shown that the people who are best adapted have strategies focused on solving problems instead of on their emotional response only.

9. What is a problem-solving approach?

It is a logical process, whereby a stressful situation is analyzed and different solutions are explored. The steps are:

1) **First step: Define the problem**. Define the problem in simple, clear and concrete terms.

2) **Second step: Seek out solutions**. Imagine as many solutions as possible, without being overly self-critical.

3) **Third step: Evaluate every possible solution**. Look at the advantages and disadvantages of each solution. Organize them according to the ease or difficulty of application and your intention of putting them into action immediately.

4) **Fourth step: Prepare a plan of action**. Decide which of the solutions you will keep as your goal. Prepare a plan of action that defines the concrete steps that need to be made.

10. What daily coping strategies can help manage stress related to emotions?

- o Learn how to express negative emotions appropriately, both to yourself and to others.
- o Avoid belittling yourself or over-dramatizing; try to perceive the real situation accurately.
- o Rely on some positive self-affirmations to control any emotions that are paralyzing (for example, "I can do it", "I've made it through worse than this", "Everything's okay, this is a step in the right direction").
- o Practice relaxation techniques to reduce the symptoms of stress.

11. What daily coping strategies can help manage stress related to behaviour?

- o Express your needs, while respecting the needs of others.
- o Avoid passively submitting to events and living like a victim of circumstance.
- o Learn to say no when you truly cannot or do not want to say yes.
- o Do not allow problems to accumulate.
- o Temporarily remove yourself from stressful situations.

12. What daily coping strategies can help manage stress related to lifestyle?

- o Plan out a balanced program that includes regular exercise, creative and relaxing activities.
- o Seek out activities that you find fulfilling and pleasurable.
- o Organize your time and establish realistic deadlines.
- o Maintain some distance between your professional life and your personal life.
- o Do not seek to deal with your stress by consuming alcohol or food to excess or by using drugs.

13. What attitudes and behaviours can help people with diabetes manage stress related to their illness?

1) **Manage the illness well:**
   - check blood glucose regularly;
   - eat well;
   - exercise;
   - take medications as prescribed;
   - learn about diabetes.

2) **Deal with external stressors:**
   - practice time management (plan, define priorities);
   - change environments, if necessary;
   - engage in satisfying activities;
   - use relaxation techniques;
   - put things in motion as soon as possible;
   - make changes gradually; avoid "all-or-nothing" reactions.

3) **Deal with psychological stressors:**
   - control irrational thoughts (for example, perfectionism);
   - question your beliefs (for example, "What I don't know can't hurt me, so I think about diabetes as little as possible");
   - open yourself up to other ways of seeing (for example, instead of seeing life in black and white, open yourself up to shades of grey);
   - build a social support network (family, friends, outreach groups) and let them know that you appreciate their support (avoid making members of your family responsible for your treatment);
   - speak with a person you trust, sharing your emotions; confiding in someone is an effective way to feel better and combat any feelings of isolation that are caused by the illness;
   - consult a specialist if your own resources seem inadequate. A psychologist is a specialist in human behaviour, and can help you identify the sources of your stress and your reactions, and change your attitudes and behaviour to better manage stress.

14. What is relaxation?

Relaxation is an important tool in stress management. Stress provokes a number of reactions, stimulating several physiological functions (cardiovascular, respiratory, muscular). Relaxation, on the other hand, produces the opposite effect with respect to these functions, re-establishing physiological and psychological equilibrium. Relaxation is more than just "rest"; its effect is deeper.

15. Are there any easy relaxation exercises?

There are a number of easy techniques. The most common are:
1) active relaxation, which involves alternating tension and release;
2) passive relaxation, which involves gradually relaxing each part of the body as each one is named inwardly.

The important thing is to stop, get away from external stimuli (noise, light, activity), sit down, close your eyes and breathe deeply, finding your own rhythm. After a few minutes, your breathing will slow down. Then conduct an inventory of every part of your body, starting at the feet and moving up to the head. You will begin to feel more relaxed, with sensations of warmth, heaviness and calm overtaking you. With practice, five minutes will be enough to attain this relaxation state anywhere, even in public places. It is just a matter of practice; it's easy, accessible to anyone and, above all, very effective.

16. Are there any tools that promote relaxation?

There is a wide variety of CDs that provide information on relaxation techniques. Experiment and explore to discover your preferences.

Here are some suggestions for beginners:
  o *Progressive Relaxation and Breathing.* 1987. Oakland, CA: New Harbinger Publications Inc. Jacobson's complete Deep Muscle Technique, shorthand relaxation of muscle groups, deep breathing, etc.
  o *Applied Relaxation Training.* 1991. Oakland, CA: New Harbinger Publications Inc. How to relax all your muscles except those you actually need for a given activity, to reduce stress while driving, working at a desk or walking.

There are also a number of books on relaxation techniques and stress management. Browse through a bookstore to find something that is appealing to you. The following is one recommendation to get you started:

- o   Martha Davis *et al.*, *Relaxation and Stress Reduction Workbook*, 5th ed. Oakland, CA: New Harbinger Publications, 2001.

17. Should you talk about your disease with your family and friends?

It is important to realize that your family and friends will share your feelings of shock, especially when you are first diagnosed. It is important to speak with them. They are worried about you and need information to help you properly. Communication is always the best choice. Your role involves instructing your family and friends, providing them with general information about diabetes, your lifestyle regimen and any possible complications. This will ensure that you get the appropriate aid and support. Expressing your needs and expectations is the first step toward mutual understanding and a way to ensure your safety.

18. What reactions should you expect from your family and friends?

In most cases, family and friends want to help, but they do not always do so in the right way. You may sometimes get the impression that they all want to tell you what you should and should not do, or that they minimize the seriousness of the illness and lure you away from what you should be doing. It is important to inform your loved ones and let them know what you need and expect. You are an autonomous person and it is normal for you to want to exert as much control over your life as possible.

19. Should you talk about your condition at work?

It is important to find allies who can help you in an emergency. You are responsible for creating a climate of safety around yourself. Your stress level will depend greatly on how successful you are at doing this.

The Motivation to Change

1. What is motivation?

Motivation is the action of conscious and unconscious forces that determine behaviour.

For example, smoking is behaviour that is determined and conditioned by a number of forces, including advertising, fashion, relaxation, or emotional conflict.

Analyzing the reasons we come up with for continuing or changing behaviour can help us become aware of these forces.

2. Why is motivation important in the treatment of diabetes?

First and foremost, motivation is an important issue in the treatment of diabetes because the disease requires people to care for themselves (self-care) and control their own blood glucose levels (self-monitoring).

Self-care and self-monitoring only work if people change their lifestyle and choose to eat better, exercise and manage their stress.

The requirements of the treatment of diabetes demand a great deal of personal motivation to adopt and maintain healthy behaviour.

3. What are the main factors behind the motivation to change?

There are three main factors:

1) **The will to change**

   In large part, the will to change is determined by personal beliefs about health, diabetes, and the treatment of the disease.

   The collection of opinions known as "health beliefs" has been shown to positively influence a person to adopt healthy behaviours (for example, the belief that the proposed treatment regimen is effective).

   On the other hand, there are also erroneous beliefs, which are very personal perceptions of the disease and its treatment that can negatively affect the will to change.

2) **The steps toward change**

   Any transformation is accomplished step by step, each one defined by the feeling of being more or less ready to take action. For each step toward change, there are recommendations about how to continue progressing.

3) **Confidence in the capacity to change**

   A person's confidence in his or her capacity to change can be reinforced by learning skills that make change easier to envisage.

   Two such skills are the manner of setting goals and familiarity with the plan or strategy for change.

4. How do the health beliefs of people with diabetes reinforce the will to change?

Health beliefs are a collection of beliefs that a person holds about diabetes and treatment. They can play a positive role in reinforcing the will to change behaviour.

The more closely health beliefs are adhered to, the stronger the will to adopt behaviours that promote good health (eating better, checking blood glucose regularly, etc.). To assess the sincerity of your will to change, do the following exercise. Ask yourself how much you really believe:

1) that you really do have diabetes;
2) that the disease can have serious consequences;
3) that following the advice of your healthcare providers will benefit your health;
4) that the benefits of treatment balance out the limitations it imposes;
5) that you feel capable of putting the advice of caregivers into action.

5. Can erroneous beliefs about the illness and its treatment be obstacles to the will to change?

Of course. Erroneous beliefs, forged from false information, rumours, family stories and cultural perceptions, are a negative influence. They are often used as justifications to avoid taking proper care of oneself, to administer inadequate treatment, or to abandon a poorly understood treatment.

Most common erroneous beliefs among people with diabetes

o If I take pills to treat diabetes, I can eat whatever I want.
o My diabetes is minor or my sugar levels are just a little bit high; I therefore don't need treatment.
o I have to eliminate all sugars from my diet.
o Taking drugs to treat diabetes creates an addiction because the drugs are "chemicals". They should be taken as little as possible.
o If I inject insulin, I will become a "junkie".
o I got diabetes because I ate too much sugar.
o Diabetes treated with insulin is much worse than diabetes treated with oral antidiabetic medications.
o My diabetes is cured because my glucose level has returned to normal.
o Since I don't have any obvious symptoms, I must not have the disease.
o If I ignore the problems, they will disappear.
o No matter what I do, I'm still going to end up with complications and dying.

---

6. What can be done to reinforce the positive effects of health beliefs and reduce the negative effects of erroneous beliefs?

1) Review your health beliefs regularly.
2) Question your personal convictions about diabetes and treatment regularly.
3) Seek out information:
   o   read up on diabetes;
   o   speak to your doctor;
   o   follow a training course at a diabetes teaching center;
   o   exchange information with other people with diabetes.

7. What are the steps to changing behaviour?

The following chart presents the steps that must be taken when changing behaviour. Being familiar with these steps can help you to identify what you need to do to get from one stage to the next.

Step	Description	Action
Pre-contemplation	You have no intention of changing your behaviour.	1) Remain open. 2) Seek out information that can make you more aware of the importance of the changes you have to make.
Contemplation	You have started to think about making changes over the next six months.	1) Determine the obstacles to change. 2) Assess the advantages and disadvantages of change. 3) Ask the people around you for help.
Preparation	You have decided to make a change over the coming month.	1) Draw up a plan, setting clear goals. 2) It can be useful to set up a verbal agreement with your doctor or diabetes health care professional. Also speak to your spouse or significant other.
Action	You have made a change. You have maintained it for fewer than six months.	Seek support, especially during periods when you feel more vulnerable, such as during vacations or periods of high stress.
Maintenance	You have made a change. You have maintained it for six months.	Reward yourself if you have achieved your goal (for example, treat yourself to a massage or set aside some money for a night out).

8. How can you set achievable goals?

The following is a list of elements to take into account to increase the likelihood of reaching your goals. Goals should be:

1) **specific:**

   The plan must be clear. For example, instead of saying "I will eat more regularly", it is better to specifically say "I will eat three meals a day, five out of every seven days".

2) **measurable:**
   It is easier to assess your progress when your goals can be checked or measured.

3) **self-directed:**
   You must participate in establishing the goals. They are yours, after all.

4) **realistic:**
   Plan your progress in small steps. Success breeds success.

5) **limited in time:**
   Decide on a starting date, a time limit and how often you will keep track of your progress.

6) **assessed in terms of the expected support:**
   Determine whether you need the support of your family, friends or caregivers to reach your goal.

9. What strategies can motivate you to exercise more?

1) **Exercise with a goal in mind:**
   Walk the dog or ride a bicycle to work, for example.

2) **Start off moderately:**
   It is better to walk only ten minutes a day than not at all.

3) **Remind yourself of the benefits of the exercise:**
   Exercise has been shown to be an excellent way to combat stress and depression and to protect from heart disease. It also helps control blood glucose levels in people with diabetes.

4) **Make exercise a regular part of your life:**
   Program your exercise regimen the way you program your work schedule or your social activities.

5) **Be flexible:**
   Do exercises that are accessible; when planning your activities, take into account your schedule, budget and abilities.

6) **Make it enjoyable:**
   Vary your physical activities to learn which ones you enjoy the most.

7) **Exercise with other people:**
   Find partners to walk, play tennis or go bird-watching with.

10. What strategies can motivate you to eat better?

Following the meal plan is probably the most difficult part of diabetes treatment. Here are a number of suggestions to help you succeed[1].

1) Develop a clear and realistic meal plan with your dietician.

2) Exert control over your environment to make it easier. For example, do not buy cookies if you know you cannot resist them.

3) Keep things in perspective if you seem to fall short of your expectations. For example, use glycosylated hemogoblin instead of just the week's blood glucose levels to assess the impact of weight loss on the control of your diabetes.

4) Beware of being too strict and depriving yourself; this can provoke an urge to abandon all your efforts.

5) Focus on the new habits you need to develop instead of the old ones you need to leave behind.

6) If your day-to-day life seems boring to you and eating has become your only pleasant and stimulating activity, you have to put some serious thought into reorganizing things. There are many options, such as volunteering or picking up a hobby.

7) Develop self-affirmation skills, especially if you are someone who finds it difficult to say "no".

1. Taken from *Diabetes Burnout* by W. Polonsky. Alexandria VA; American Diabetes Association, 1999.

Sex and Family Planning

1. Can diabetes affect the sex lives of people with diabetes?

Diabetes can cause problems affecting sexuality in both men and women. In women, these problems are less obvious and do not directly impede the sex act. It is worth noting, however, that there has been less research into the problems experienced by women and they are therefore less understood. As for men, on the other hand, chronic elevated blood glucose can cause difficulty in achieving and maintaining an erection and therefore the inability to have satisfactory sexual relations: this is known as **erectile dysfunction.**

2. Do all men with diabetes suffer from erectile dysfunction?

No. Not all men with diabetes necessarily develop erectile dysfunction.

3. How does diabetes cause erectile dysfunction in men?

In the long term, hyperglycemia can cause two problems:
1) nerve damage;
2) thickening and hardening of the arteries, which can hamper circulation.

These two problems, either separately or in combination, can lead to the partial or complete inability to achieve erection (erectile dysfunction).

Poorly controlled diabetes and an illness affecting general health can also cause erectile dysfunction. In such a case, correcting hyperglycemia generally enables a return of normal sexual function.

4. **When men with diabetes have erectile dysfunction, is it always caused by the disease?**
    No. Erectile dysfunction in men with diabetes is often due to causes that have nothing to do with the disease. Possible causes include:
    1) medications;
    2) hormonal problems;
    3) psychological problems.

5. **How can men with diabetes prevent erectile dysfunction?**
    The risk of erectile dysfunction can be reduced by:
    1) keeping blood glucose levels as close to normal as possible;
    2) following the meal plan's recommendations on fats;
    3) quitting smoking, if applicable;
    4) maintaining control of high blood pressure and any blood lipid abnormalities;
    5) stopping or decreasing alcohol consumption, if applicable.

6. **How is erectile dysfunction assessed?**
    The following tests are performed to assess erectile dysfunction:
    1) Doppler test to measure penile blood flow;
    2) electromyography (EMG) of the penis to measure neurological conductivity;
    3) measurement of hormone levels;
    4) evaluation of nocturnal erections; the occurrence of nocturnal erections suggests the problem has a psychological origin;
    5) psychological evaluation if these tests are negative.

7. **Can erectile dysfunction be treated in men with diabetes?**
    Yes. The key is to identify the problem in order to find the appropriate treatment:
    1) better control of blood glucose can help in some cases;
    2) any hormonal problems should be corrected;
    3) any drugs that disturb sexual function should be eliminated, if possible;
    4) in some cases, drugs can be used to induce erection and eventually make full sexual relations possible:
        o   medications taken orally, such as Viagra®, Cialis® or Levitra®;

o   insertion of prostaglandin suppositories (Muse®) into the urethra;

o   injection of prostaglandin at the base of the penis (Caverject®);

5)   in the case of severe organic erectile dysfunction, a penile prosthetic device can be used;

6)   sex therapy is often useful; it can either help the person adapt to his sexual difficulties or resolve any psychological conflicts that are at the root of the sexual problem.

8.   Are there any risks associated with pregnancy in women with diabetes?

Yes. Pregnancy can cause certain risks for women with diabetes, especially if blood glucose is poorly controlled. There are three types of risk:

1)   **risks to the mother:**

o   aggravation of the complications of diabetes;

o   urinary infections;

o   acidosis in women with type 1 diabetes;

o   severe hypoglycemia.

2)   **risks to the baby:**

o   spontaneous miscarriage;

o   malformation;

o   death in utero;

o   premature birth;

o   hypoglycemia at birth.

3)   **risks to both mother and baby:**

o   toxemia of pregnancy, characterized by high blood pressure, protein in the urine and edema of the lower limbs;

o   macrosomia (excessive birth weight of more then 4 kg at full term).

The risk of complications is significantly reduced if blood glucose is properly controlled both before and during pregnancy.

9.   How can women with diabetes prevent complications associated with pregnancy?

Complications can generally be avoided. It is essential for a woman with diabetes to **consult her doctor** before deciding to become pregnant. It is very important to:

1) assess and treat any complications that could worsen during pregnancy, especially if they involve the eyes;
2) control blood glucose, prior to conception, as much as possible to reduce the risk of congenital malformation.

A woman with diabetes should consider becoming pregnant only once these issues have been addressed.

10. Are there risks of complications during pregnancy in women with diabetes?

Yes. Some of the complications related to diabetes carry high risks for pregnant women, especially if blood glucose is poorly controlled:
1) progression of retinopathy;
2) progression of kidney damage with severe loss of renal function;
3) severe high blood pressure;
4) heart failure if there is prior heart damage.

If these complications develop, it may be necessary to consider a **therapeutic termination of the pregnancy.**

11. What are the risks of a child developing diabetes if one of the parents has the disease?

If one of the parents has **type 1 diabetes,** the long-term risk of the child developing diabetes is **5%.** The risk is higher if the father has diabetes.

If one of the parents has **type 2 diabetes,** the long-term risk of the baby developing diabetes is **25%.**

12. What contraceptive methods are available to women with diabetes?

There are no contraceptive methods specifically designed for women with diabetes. Some methods do carry greater risks for these women, however.

There are two types of contraceptives:

1) **hormonal contraceptives:**
    - o **combined birth control pills,** which contain two hormones, estrogen and progestin. They are effective, but they carry certain risks for blood glucose levels and blood vessels. There is also a skin patch and a vaginal ring that releases a combination of estrogen and progestin;
    - o **low-dose progestin pills,** which contain a small amount of progestin. They are effective and have little impact on blood glucose, but their long-term effect on blood vessels is unknown;
    - o intramuscular injections of progestin or intra-uterine devices (IUDs) with progestin. They are effective and have no impact on blood glucose or on blood vessels;

2) **mechanical contraception:**
    - o intra-uterine devices (IUDs) are effective and present no risk of infection, provided blood glucose levels are properly controlled;
    - o localized methods such as condoms, diaphragms and spermicide can be used by women with diabetes without risk.

The choice of method should be guided by the woman's age, how long she has had diabetes, how well it is managed, whether there are complications, whether she smokes, how many times she has been pregnant before, the effectiveness of the contraceptive, and above all, the preferences of the woman and her partner.

13. Can a woman with diabetes use emergency oral contraception (the "morning-after pill")?

Emergency oral contraception, which is used after unprotected sexual intercourse, is not contraindicated for women with diabetes. On the other hand, it is not recommended for regular use. It involves taking an oral contraceptive in one of the following ways:

1) a 100 μg dose of ethinylestradiol (an estrogen) combined with 500 μg of levonorgestrel (a progestin) as soon as possible after intercourse, and a second dose 12 hours later (for example, two doses of two Ovral® tablets); or

2) one dose of 750 μg of levonorgestrel (Plan B®) as soon as possible after intercourse and a second dose 12 hours later.

Emergency oral contraception should be prescribed by a doctor or, in Quebec, by a doctor or pharmacist.

14. What sterilization methods are available to women with diabetes and their partners?

Sterilization is an option that is worth considering when women with the disease have been pregnant a number of times, especially if they have experienced complications related to diabetes. The options are:

1) tubal ligation, for the woman;
2) vasectomy, for the man.

15. Can a menopausal woman with diabetes take hormones?

Menopausal women with diabetes can take estrogen, either with or without progestin. It has recently been demonstrated, however, that combined hormonal therapy (estrogen and progestin) in menopausal women is associated with a minimal but significant risk of breast cancer, thrombophlebitis (blood clots), strokes and heart disease. Menopausal women should therefore only take hormones (estrogen and progestin) if menopausal symptoms are difficult (for example, hot flashes) and only for a maximum of four years. Afterwards, medication should be discontinued if the symptoms are gone.

When deciding whether to take estrogen, the following high-risk situations should be taken into account:

1) prior thrombophlebitis;
2) prior cerebrovascular problems, especially in women who smoke;
3) a history of breast cancer.

Community Resources

This book was written by the multidisciplinary team of the Diabetes Day-Care Unit of the CHUM Hôtel-Dieu Hospital.

The CHUM Hôtel-Dieu diabetes day unit opened its doors in March 1995 in response to a need for education, research and development in the area of diabetes.

Every week, the Diabetes Day-Care unit welcomes about a dozen people and their families for a four-day training session. Individual and group encounters give people an opportunity to learn more about every aspect of diabetes. This type of knowledge can help people with diabetes become more independent with respect to their illness.

A multidisciplinary team of endocrinologists, nurses, dieticians, and psychologists offers the following training programs to people with diabetes:

- four-day course (regular program) of workshops and individual evaluations;
- two-day course (intensive program) of workshops;
- one-day refresher every six months (after initial training);
- four hours a month for amblyopic or blind people;
- four hours a month for people with cystic fibrosis.

Everything is offered free of charge, and every person with diabetes receives a copy of the book *Understand Your Diabetes and Live a Healthy Life.*

Recommendations are sent to the treating physician for the four-day course.

All interested parties can contact:

Diabetes Day-Care Unit
CHUM Hôtel-Dieu
3840 Saint-Urbain Street
Montreal, Quebec H2W 1T8
Tel.: 514 890-8000, extension 14658

There are a number of other diabetes teaching centres accessible through the health network. The Diabetes Québec magazine *Plein Soleil* and the Diabetes Québec website contain a list of these centres. The local branches of the Canadian Diabetes Association, present in all provinces except Quebec, are also a valuable source of information.

Physical Activity

1. **What exercise services and facilities are available to people with diabetes?**

    Amicale des diabétiques des hôpitaux Notre-Dame et Maisonneuve-Rosemont
    (aquafitness, gentle conditioning, group walking)
    2065 Alexandre-de-Sève Street
    9th floor, suite Z-9903-4
    Montreal, Quebec H2L 2W5
    Tel.: 514 890-8000, extension 25358
    E-mail: amicale.diabetique.chum@ssss.gouv.qc.ca

    Centre ÉPIC
    5055 Saint-Zotique Street East
    Montreal, Quebec H1T 1N6
    Tel.: 514 374-1480
    Fax: 514 374-2445
    Website: www.icm-mhi.org

Clinique de kinésiologie
CEPSUM–Université de Montréal
2100 Édouard-Montpetit Blvd., suite 205
C. P. 6128, Succ. Centre-ville
Montreal, Quebec H3C 3J7
Tel.: 514 343-6150
Fax: 514 343-2188
E-mail: cliniquekin@kinesio.umontreal.ca
Website: www.kinesio.umontreal.ca
www.cepsum.umontreal.ca

Centre de santé et de services sociaux Jeanne-Mance
Health motivation education centre
1051 Saint-Hubert Street
Montreal, Quebec H2L 3Y5
Tel.: 514 521-7663, extension 6559
Website: www.santemontreal.qc.ca/csss/jeannemance

Fédération québécoise de la marche
Marche-Randonnée **magazine**
4545 Pierre-de-Coubertin Avenue
C.P. 1000, succ. M
Montreal, Quebec H1V 3R7
Tel.: 514 252-3157 or toll-free 1 866 252-2065
Fax : 514 252-5137
Website: www.fqmarche.qc.ca

Outdoor recreational activity groups (for people who are more active)
www.actionpassion.com
www.aventuremonde.com
www.azimutaventure.com/
www.bougex.com
www.horizonroc.com/
www.aventuriers.qc.ca
www.cycloconcept.ca
www.cyclonature.org

www.detournature.com
www.karavaniers.com
www.groupeoxygene.qc.ca
www.pulsations.ca
www.passionaventure.com

Kino-Québec
www.kino-quebec.qc.ca
www.actimetre.qc.ca (adult physical activity assessment software and recommendations)

Socioeconomic support

2.   **What kind of socioeconomic support is available?**
   o   **Access to welfare**
       People with diabetes who are eligible for welfare receive an additional $20 per month. They must communicate with the agent responsible for their file for further information.
       •   Solidarité sociale, Bureau des renseignements et plaintes
           Tel. toll-free: 1 888 643-4721

   o   **Family allowance**
       An extra $167 per month is added to the family allowance for parents with a dependent child who has diabetes. The request for the supplement must be filled out and signed by the pediatrician.
       •   Régie des rentes du Québec
           Tel.: 514 864-3873 or 1 800 667-9625 (benefits for handicapped children)

   o   **Régie des rentes du Québec**
       Tel.: 514 864-3873 or 1 800 667-9625 (benefits for han dicapped children)

   o   **Tax credit**
       People with chronic diseases requiring daily care may be entitled to a federal tax credit.

o   **Loans and Bursaries**

Full-time CEGEP or university students with diabetes are reimbursed for the cost of their medication.

Students must make a loan and bursary request at the financial aid office of their school and follow the steps set out in the program.

The cost of medications is reimbursed by the Ministère de l'Éducation, according to the *Act respecting financial assistance for education expenses*. Tel.: 418 643-3750 or toll-free 1 877 643-3750

Insurance

3. What factors should people with diabetes consider when taking out insurance?

Important facts
- Insurance taken out before the diagnosis of diabetes remains in force under the same terms.
- When a new application for insurance is made, people with diabetes must undergo a medical assessment to determine their new level of risk. Each person with diabetes is considered as a separate case.
- In the case of mortgage life insurance, the benefit is usually not available if the diabetes is pre-existing or if the disease is diagnosed before the renewal of the policy.

Group insurance
- Like all other employees, people with diabetes benefit from compulsory coverage. People with diabetes may take out optional coverage with no additional premium if the request is made before the imposed deadline. Beyond the deadline, coverage is usually refused.
- When a person leaves a particular employment, group insurance policies can often be converted into individual insurance.

Individual life insurance

- People with diabetes should consult with several insurance companies before signing a contract. Every insurer has its own method of evaluation.
- There are many possible types of insurance for people with diabetes:
  - additional premiums that vary widely, possibly increasing from one year to the next; the premium depends on each individual's risk assessment
  - "health option" flat rate, where the admissibility and maintenance of the protection depends on criteria related to how well the diabetes is controlled.

Associations

4. What associations provide support to people with diabetes?

Canadian Diabetes Association
1400-522 University Avenue
Toronto, Ontario M5G 2R5
Tel.: 1 800 226-8464
Website: www.diabetes.ca
Magazine : *Diabetes Dialogue*

American Diabetes Association
1701 North Beauregard Street
Alexandria, VA 22311
United States of America
Tel.: 1 800 342-2383
Website: www.diabetes.org
Magazine: *Diabetes Forecast*

Diabetes Québec
8550 Pie-IX Blvd., suite 300
Montreal, Quebec H1Z 4G2
Tel.: 514 259-3422 or 1 800 361-3504
E-mail: info@diabete.qc.ca
Website: www.diabete.qc.ca
Magazine: *Plein soleil*

Blind or Amblyopic

5. **What services are offered to people with diabetes who are blind or amblyopic?**

Philips Lifeline
Remote surveillance (two-way vocal communicator)
774 Décarie Blvd., suite 100
Saint-Laurent, Quebec H4L 3L5
Tel.: 514 735-2101 or 1 877 423-9700
Website: www.lifeline.ca

Montreal Association for the Blind
7000 Sherbrooke Street West
Montreal, Quebec H4B 1R3
Tel.: 514 489-8201
Fax: 514 489-3477
Website: www.mab.ca

Institut de réadaptation en déficience physique du Québec
525 Wilfrid-Hamel Blvd., Wing J
Quebec City, Quebec G1M 2S8
Tel.: 418 529-9141
Fax: 418 529-3699
Website: www.irdpq.qc.ca

Canadian National Institute for the Blind
2015 Peel Street, suite 460
Montreal, Quebec H3A 1T8
Tel: 514 934-4622 or 1 800 465-4622
Fax: 514-934-2131
Website: www.inca.ca

Institut Nazareth et Louis-Braille
1111 Saint-Charles Street West
Longueuil, Quebec J4K 5G4
Tel.: 450 463-1710 or 1 800 361-7063
Fax: 450 463-0243
Website: www.inlb.qc.ca

Specialized equipment for amblyopic or visually impaired people
- Braille blood glucose notebook
  CHUM Hôtel-Dieu diabetes day unit
  Tel.: 514 890-8000, extension 14658
- CD for people who are visually impaired
  - Diabetes Québec
    Plein soleil magazine
    Tel.: 514 259-3422 or 1 800 361-3504
  - CHUM Hôtel-Dieu Diabetes day-care unit
    1) *Understand Your Diabetes and Live a Healthy Life*
    2) Recipes with calculated carbohydrates for the visually impaired: *Recettes faciles pour diabétiques et semi-voyants 2006*
      Distributed by the Service québécois du livre adapté
      Tel.: 514 873-4454 or 1 866 410-0844
- Blood glucose metres
  - **Bayer Ascensia® Contour** ® with speech synthesis
    distributed by Pharmacie Danielle Desroches
    Tel.: 514 288-8555 or 450 447-9280
  - **Accu-Chek® Compact Plus®** from Roche Diagnostics
    A reader emitting beeps; model with speech synthesis
    Tel.: 1 800 363-7949

- Syringe support for the blind
  Institut de réadaptation en déficience physique du Québec
  Tel.: 418 529-9141

Regroupement des aveugles et amblyopes du Montréal métropolitain
5215 Berri Street, suite 200
Montreal, Quebec H2J 2S4
Tel.: 514 277-4401
Fax: 514 277-8961
Website: www.raamm.org

Service québécois du livre adapté
475 de Maisonneuve Blvd. East
Montreal, Quebec H2L 5C4
514 873-4454 or 1 866 410-0844
Website: www.banq.qc.ca/portal/dt/sqla/sqla.htm

Diabetes Québec

6.   What services are offered by Diabetes Québec?

Diabète Québec
8550 Pie-IX Blvd., suite 300
Montreal (Quebec) H1Z 4G2
Tel.: 514 259-3422 or toll-free 1 800 361-3504
Website: www.diabete.qc.ca
Email: info@diabete.qc.ca

Diabetes Québec is a non-profit association bringing people with diabetes and health professionals together. Its mission is education, sensitization, and prevention. There are four general aspects to the work done by this organization: training, encouraging research, defending the rights of people with diabetes, and ensuring that services are provided. Some of its services are free, while others are offered at a nominal price.

○ The *Plein soleil* magazine, which features useful information about diabetes;
○ lectures;
○ educational materials (books, brochures, and the videocassette entitled "Foot Care for Diabetics");
○ training tailored to specific groups of people with diabetes and health professionals;
○ an information phone line:
InfoDiabetes
Tel.: 514 259-3422, extension 233 or toll-free 1 800 361-3504
E-mail: infodiabete@diabete.qc.ca

Grieving

7. What bereavement services are available to people with diabetes?

Services commémoratifs Mont-Royal
(sharing and discussion groups on bereavement)
1297 Chemin de la Forêt
Outremont, Quebec H2V 2P9
Tel.: 514 279-7358
Fax: 514 279-0049
Website: www.mountroyalcem.com

Vie nouvelle (information about the grieving process and discussion groups)
Verdun Hospital
4000 LaSalle Blvd., Suite 5114
Montreal, Quebec H4G 2A3
Tel.: 514 362-1000, extension 2883
Fax: 514 362-7402

Children

8. What services are offered to children with diabetes?

Camp pour enfants diabétiques de l'est du Québec

11 Crémazie Street East

Quebec City, Quebec G1R 1Y1

Tel.: 418 523-6159

E-mail: info@cedeq.org

Website: www.cedeq.org

Juvenile Diabetes Research Foundation

2155 Guy Street, suite 1120

Montreal, Quebec H3H 2R9

Tel.: 514 744-5537 or 1 877 634-2238

Fax: 514 744-0516

E-mail: montreal@jdrf.ca

Website: www.jdrf.ca

The Diabetic Children's Foundation and Camp Carowanis

785 Plymouth Street, suite 210

Mont-Royal, Quebec H4P 1B3

Tel.: 514731-9683 or 514 731-9683 or 1 800 731-9683

Fax: 514 731-2683

E-mail: carowanis@diabete-enfants.ca

Website: www.diabetes-children.ca

Medical Identification

9. **Where can I get a medical bracelet or pendant?**

Jewellery stores

Canadian Medic-Alert Foundation
2005, Sheppard Avenue East, suite 800
Toronto, Ontario M2J 5B4
Tel.: 416 696-0267 or 1 800 668-6381
Website: www.medicalert.ca

Pharmacies

Feet

10. **What foot care services are available?**

Association des infirmières et infirmiers en soins de pieds du Québec
3850 Jean-Talon Street West, Suite 122
Montreal, Quebec H3R 2G8
Tel.: 514 344-7212 or toll-free 1 800 771-9664
Fax: 514 344-0766
E-mail: info@aiispq.qc.ca

Clinique d'évaluation et de traitement podologique pour patients atteints de diabète (pied diabétique)
CHUM Hôtel-Dieu
3840 Saint-Urbain Street
Montreal, Quebec H2W 1T8
Tel.: 514 890-8151 (make an appointment at Centre des rendez-vous)

Ordre des podiatres du Québec
300 Saint-Sacrement Street, Suite 102
Montreal, Quebec H2Y 1X4
Tel.: 514 288-0019
Website: www.ordredespodiatres.qc.ca

Driver's Licence

11. What factors should people with diabetes consider when getting a driver's licence?

Important facts

- Diabetes can cause problems that affect visual sharpness and field of vision. Obviously, vision plays a fundamental role in driving an automobile.
- Driving is a **privilege**, not **a right to be taken for granted** or bestowed without reservation.
- The SAAQ (Société de l'assurance automobile du Québec) establishes the rules governing the acquisition and holding of this privilege. These rules revolve around a person's ability to **drive safely**, as regards himself or herself and all others. The state of the driver's health is taken into account.

Medical assessment

- A medical assessment form is sent out to people with diabetes at varying intervals.
- The report must be filled out by the treating doctor and/or optometrist within the time frame specified (three months).

> The SAAQ medical assessment takes into account how well the diabetes is controlled.

The SAAQ bases its decision on this medical opinion. It places more weight on functional limitations than on the diagnosis.

Hypoglycemia and driving

- Hypoglycemia can compromise the ability of a person with diabetes to drive safely. It occurs most often in people with diabetes who are treated with insulin and less frequently in those who take medications to stimulate the production of insulin (sulfonylureas, meglitinides).
- Necessary preventive measures include the following:
  - always have rapidly absorbed sugars nearby;
  - avoid driving for long periods without a break;
  - never skip meals or snacks;
  - carry an emergency food supply in case a meal is delayed.

Legal obligations

The law provides the following:

- Holders of a **driver's licence are under a legal obligation** to inform the SAAQ of any disease or change that is, in particular, related to their physical and mental health when they first apply for their permit and within 30 days of the change in their health. Knowingly providing false or misleading information is an offence and can lead to the suspension of the person's driver's licence and a fine.
- Holders of a driver's licence are under a legal obligation to respond to a request for a medical report within the specified time.

> Any person providing false or misleading information is guilty of an offence and may be subject to prosecution. A false declaration renders the driver fully responsible, which could have serious repercussions in the case of an accident.

For more information, contact the Service de l'évaluation médicale at the SAAQ:

> Service de l'évaluation médicale, SAAQ
> P.O. 19500,
> Quebec City, Quebec G1K 8J5
> Tel.: 418 643-5506 or toll-free 1 800 561-2858
> Website: www.saaq.qc.ca

Professionals

12. What nutritional resources are available to people with diabetes?

Dieticians

- **Association des diététistes au Québec**
  Tel.: 514 954-0047
  Fax: 514 932-8108
  Website: www.adaqnet.org

- **Ordre professionnel des diététistes du Québec**
  2155 Guy Street, Suite 1220
  Montreal, Quebec H3H 2R9
  Tel.: 514 393-3733 or toll-free 1 888- 393-8528
  Website: www.opdq.org

Books about diabetes and nutrition

- Isabelle Galibois, *Le diabète de type 1 et ses défis alimentaires quotidiens* (Quebec City: Les Presses de l'Université Laval, 2005).

Cookbooks with carbohydrate counts

- Anne Lindsay, *Smart Cooking: Quick and Tasty Recipes for Healthy Living* (Canadian Cancer Society, 1997).

- *Anne Lindsay's Light Kitchen* (Wiley, 1991)

- Anne Lindsay, in collaboration with Denise Beatty of the Canadian Medical Association, *Anne Lindsay's New Light Kitchen* (Random House Canada, 1998).

- Manon Poissant, Céline Raymond & Josée Rouette, *La nouvelle cuisine santé* (Éditions Stanké, 1998).

- Karen Graham, *Meals for Good Health* (Canadian Diabetes Association, 2005).

- Manon Robitaille & Daniel Lavoie, *Le dessert se fait léger* (Éditions Diabète Québec, 2007).

- N. Delisle, M. Forget & S. Larouche, *Les sucres et pourquoi pas* (Métro Richelieu et Diabète Québec, 2001).

- N. Delisle, M. Forget & S. Larouche, *Les sucres… Question d'équilibre* (Éditions Profil-Santé, 2007).

- Helen Bishop, et al., *Eat Well, Live Well: The Canadian Dietetic Association's Guide to Healthy Eating.*, (Macmillan of Canada, 1990).

- Katherine E. Younker, *The Best Diabetes Cookbook* (published in cooperation with the Canadian Diabetes Association, R. Rose, 2005.)

- *Qu'est-ce qu'on mange?* Vol. 4. (Cercle des fermières du Québec, 1997)

- Various authors, *Simplement délicieux*, Éditions du Trécarré, 2007.

Web sites on diabetes and nutrition
- Recipe analyzer
  - Dieticians of Canada:
    Website: www.dietitians.ca : Eat Well, Live Well > English home > Recipe Analyzer

- Carbohydrate calculator (advanced method):
  www.diabete.qc.ca
  (for download)

- L'Épicerie television show on Radio-Canada
  www.radio-canada.ca/actualite/v2/lepicerie/

- Extenso, Centre de référence sur la nutrition humaine (information on human nutrition)
  www.extenso.org

- Fédération des producteurs maraîchers du Québec
  www.legumesduquebec.com

- Canada's Food Guide
  www.hc-sc.gc.ca/fn-an/food-guide-aliment/index-eng.php

- Passeport santé
  www.passeportsante.net

- SOS cuisine
  www.soscuisine.com

- Nutritional value of foods
  - CalorieKing
    www.calorieking.com
  - Canadian Nutrient File
    www.hc-sc.gc.ca : Food & Nutrition > Nutrition & Healthy Eating >
    Search online for food in the Canadian Nutrient file 2007b > English
  - Nutritional values of some common foods
    www.hc-sc.gc.ca : Food & Nutrition > Nutrition & Healthy Eating >
    Nutrient Data > Nutrient Value of Some Common Foods > PDF
    Version

Websites featuring recipes with carbohydrate counts
  - Association canadienne du diabète
    www.diabetes.ca> Recipes > RecipesIndex.asp
  - American Diabetes Association
    www.diabetes.org : Nutrition > MyFoodAdvisor > Recipes
  - Diabetes Québec
    www.diabete.qc.ca : Alimentation > Recettes

Nursing Services

13. What nursing care resources are available to people with diabetes?

Nurses

Ordre des infirmières et infirmiers du Québec

4200 Dorchester Blvd. West

Westmount, Quebec H3Z 1V4

Tel.: 514 935-2501 or toll-free 1 800 363-6048

Fax: 514 935-1799

E-mail: inf@oiiq.org

Website: www.oiiq.org

Info-Santé

CLSC (Quebec community health centres) telephone help line, available 24 hours a day to provide answers to health questions. Since April 2008, this service can be reached by dialing **811**.

All **CLSCs** are open from 8 a.m. to 4 p.m.

Medical services

14. How can you get medical assistance?

Collège des médecins du Québec

2170 René-Lévesque Blvd. West

Montreal, Quebec H3H 2T8

Tel.: 514 933-4441 or toll-free 1 888 633-3246

Fax: 514 933-3112

Website: www.cmq.org

DOCTORS

My family doctor: _____   Tel._____

My endocrinologist_____   Tel._____

Endocrinologist on call
at my hospital:_____   Tel._____

Pharmacists Services

15. How can you get help from a pharmacist?

Ordre des pharmaciens du Québec

266 Notre-Dame Street West, suite 301

Montreal, Quebec H2Y 1T6

Tel.: 514 284-9588 or toll-free 1 800 363-0324

Website: www.opq.org

Any pharmacy

Régime public d'assurance-médicaments (Quebec)

- Contact the Régime de l'assurance maladie du Québec
  Tel.: 1 888 435-79999
  Website: www.ramq.gouv.qc.ca

PHARMACISTS

My pharmacist: _____   Tel._____

My pharmacy: _____   Tel._____

Psychological Services

16. What psychological services are available to people with diabetes?

Psychologists

- **Ordre des psychologues du Québec**
  1100 Beaumont Avenue, suite 510
  Mont-Royal, Quebec H3P 3H5
  Tel.: 514 738-1881 or toll-free 1 800 363-2644
  Website: www.ordrepsy.qc.ca

Anxiety and mood disorders

- **Hôpital Louis-Hippolyte LaFontaine**
  7401 Hochelaga Street
  Montreal, Quebec H1N 3M5
  Note: Ask for the Evaluation-Liaison Module
  (medical reference necessary)
  Tel.: 514 251-4000, extension 2495
  Fax: 514 251-7527
  Website: www.hlhl.qc.ca

- **Anxiety disorder clinic/ Depressive disorder clinic**
  Douglas Mental Health University Institute
  6875 Lasalle Blvd.
  Montreal, Quebec H4N 1R3
  Note: Ask for the Evaluation-Liaison Module
  (medical reference necessary)
  Tel.: 514 888-4469
  Website: www.douglas.qc.ca

Services for addiction, alcohol abuse, drug abuse, and problem gambling

- **Centre Dollard-Cormier**
  950 de Louvain Street East
  Montreal, Quebec H2M 2E8
  Tel.: 514 385-1232
  Website: ww.centredollarcormier.qc.ca

Sex therapy services

17. What resources are available regarding sexual concerns related to diabetes?

Sex therapists

- **Association des sexologues du Québec**
  7400 Boul Saint Laurent, office 404
  Montreal, Quebec H2R 2Y1
  Tel.: 514 270-9289
  Website: www.associationdessexologues.com

- **Sexual Dysfunction Unit at the CHUM Hôpital St-Luc**
  Édouard-Asselin Building, 5th floor
  264 René-Lévesque Blvd. East
  Montreal, Quebec H2X 1P1
  Tel.: 514 890-8351

Websites

18. What are some useful websites on diabetes?

- Canadian Food Inspection Agency (information on food labelling and advertising)
  Tel.: 450 928-4300 or toll-free 1 800 442-2342
  www.cfia-acia.agr.ca

- American Diabetes Association
  www.diabetes.org

- American Dietetic Association
  www.webdietitians.org

- Canadian Diabetes Association
  www.diabetes.ca

o   Association de langue française pour l'étude du diabète et des maladies métaboliques
    www.alfediam.org

o   CDC Diabetes Public Health Resource
    www.cdc.gov/diabetes

o   CH Baie-des-Chaleurs
    www.chbc.qc.ca/lediabete/default.htm

o   Children with Diabetes
    www.childrenwithdiabetes.com/index_cwd.htm

o   Diabetes Québec
    www.diabete.qc.ca

o   Diabetes Insight
    www.diabetic.org.uk

o   Diabetes.com Health Library
    www.diabetes.com/tools/health_library/index.html

o   European Association for the Study of Diabetes
    www.easd.org

o   International Diabetes Federation
    www.idf.org

o   Joslin Diabetes Center
    www.joslin.harvard.edu

o   Juvenile Diabetes Research Foundation Canada
    www.jdfc.ca

o   Diabetes in Canada
    www.phac-aspc.gc.ca/publicat/dic-dac2/english/05contents_e.html

- o   Le diabète au jour le jour
    www.ciminfo.org/diabete/index.html

- o   Dieticians of Canada
    www.dietitians.ca

- o   Medline plus: diabetes
    www.nlm.nih.gov/medlineplus/diabetes.html

- o   National Diabetes Education Program
    www.ndep.nih.gov

- o   National Institute of Diabetes & Digestive & Kidney Diseases
    www.niddk.nih.gov/health/diabetes/diabetes.htm

- o   National Institutes of Health
    www.niddk.nih.gov

- o   Programme d'enseignement diabète
    www.hopitallaval.qc.ca

Smoking

19. What services are offered to people with diabetes who want to quit smoking?

Centre d'abandon du tabagisme

Free assistance and personalized support is available everywhere in Quebec.

- Speak to a specialist on the telephone on the J'Arrete line: 1-866-jarrete or 1 866 527-7383.

- Resources to help you keep your resolve are available online at www.jarrette.qc.ca.

- Meet with a professional at a Centre d'abandon du tabagisme (centre for quitting smoking) nearest you for personalized services to help you quit.

- For the address of the Centre d'abandon du tabagisme nearest you, call 1 866-jarrete or 1 866 527-7383.

- At the CHUM: to make an appointment, call 514 890-8226; for information only, call 514 890-8000, extension 15983.

Work

20. What workplace concerns should people with diabetes keep in mind?

People with diabetes should tell people at their workplace about their disease.

- The *Charter of Rights and Freedoms* protects people with diabetes against any and all discrimination.
- People with diabetes should be as candid as possible with their employer and a few select colleagues, keeping in mind workplace context (for example, it is a good idea to inform people of what to do in the event of serious hypoglycemia).

Some jobs or professions should be avoided.

- People with diabetes are discouraged from taking certain jobs:
  - for example, airplane pilot, fireman, emergency vehicle driver, high-voltage lineworkers, etc.
- Certain jobs can be difficult for people with diabetes:
  - for example, garbage collector (increased risk of infection), cook (difficult to follow the meal plan), jeweller (requires good eyesight), etc.

Workplace behaviour

- Employers or colleagues may change the way they interact with a co-worker who has diabetes when they first learn of the disease. This is a temporary and foreseeable stage of the adaptation process.
- Like everyone else, people with diabetes have the fundamental right to be full members of society. Work is one of the most important tools to help achieve personal growth and self-realization.
- The International Association of Machinists—Center for Administering Rehabilitation and Employment Services (AIM CARES) can help you. This association offers a free specialized job search service.

> 750 Marcel-Laurin Blvd., suite 450
> Saint-Laurent, Quebec H4M 2M4
> Tel.: 514 744-2944 or 514 744-2613
> E-mail: emploi@aimcroitqc.org
> Website: www.aimcroitqc.org

YOUR STRONG POINTS

People with diabetes who are looking for a job can actually take advantage of the constraints their illness imposes when they are looking for a job. People with diabetes have had to acquire a number of positive qualities including discipline, consistency, perseverance, dedication to a healthy lifestyle, and so on.

Travel

21. What services are offered to people with diabetes who want to travel?

Travel Health Clinics in Canada

Public Health Agency of Canada

Web\site: http://www.phac-aspc.gc.ca/index-eng.php

Regional Quebec office

Suite 218, Complexe Guy-Favreau

200 René-Lévesque Blvd. West, East Tower

Montreal, Quebec H2Z 1X4

Tel.: 514 283-2306

Fax: 514 283-6739

Clinique Santé-Voyage Saint-Luc (Saint-Luc Travel Health Clinic)

1001 Saint-Denis Street, 6th floor

Montreal, Québec H2X 3H9

Tel.: 514 890-8332

Fax: 514 412-7362

E-mail: info@santevoyagesaint-luc.com

Website: www.santevoyagesaint-luc.com

Research:
What the Future Holds

There have been steady advances in diabetes research over recent years. This chapter will outline the main questions that have been answered, as well as those that are still receiving the attention of researchers.

1. **What is the cause of type 1 or "juvenile" diabetes?**

   Alterations in the pancreatic beta cells, caused by environmental factors such as a viral infection, can lead to loss of recognition of one's own cells. Mistaking them for foreign cells, the body produces antibodies to destroy them. The capacity to create antibodies against its own cells has a genetic component and these antibodies can be detected approximately five years before the development of the disease.

2. **Are there ways to prevent diabetes?**

   A number of different methods have been attempted to prevent the appearance of the disease in people at high risk.

   1) treatments attempting to block the production of antibodies as soon as they appear and treatments using insulin injections or orally administered doses failed to prevent type 1 diabetes;

   2) an international nutritional study currently underway is trying to determine whether early introduction of solid foods or cow's milk to young children at risk could influence the risk of development of type 1 diabetes later on;

3) there is currently research underway into the genes involved in the development and progression of diabetes, whether type 1 or type 2. Teams from Montreal have made a number of discoveries in this area. Gene KIAA0350, which codes for a protein that binds molecules containing sugar, has been associated with type 1 diabetes. Several genes (including TCF7L2) that are involved in the development and the function of pancreatic beta cells and in metabolic mechanisms have variants that create a predisposition to type 2 diabetes in approximately 70% of cases.

3. What is the cause of type 2 diabetes?

There are two major factors involved in the development of the type 2 diabetes: insulin resistance (meaning that a great deal more insulin is required to maintain normal blood glucose levels) and a decrease in the capacity of pancreatic cells to produce the insulin. In most cases, insulin resistance precedes the development of diabetes by several years. As long as the pancreatic cells can compensate by producing more insulin, blood glucose levels remain normal. It is only once the pancreatic cells are no longer able to compensate and insulin production decreases that blood glucose levels increase. At first, blood glucose levels rise, especially after meals. This is known as impaired glucose tolerance, and it characterizes the pre-diabetic stage. If insulin production decreases further, blood glucose levels rise even higher after meals and eventually even before meals. This is diabetes proper.

4. What factors contribute to insulin resistance?

Susceptibility to insulin resistance and a lowered capacity for insulin production are in part hereditary. Excess weight and a lack of physical activity contribute to insulin resistance and an increased risk of developing diabetes. Research has shown that efforts to reduce insulin resistance in people who are glucose intolerant have significantly reduced the risk of developing diabetes.

5. What types of interventions have positive effects on the prevention of type 2 diabetes?

The ideal is to intervene as early as possible. This is quite a challenge, however, because in some cases, an increased risk for diabetes can begin before birth if the fetus is exposed to unfavourable conditions inside the uterus. Gestational diabetes in the mother and low birth weight are possible risk factors for the development of diabetes as an adult.

Some interventions have been shown to be effective in preventing type 2 diabetes:
1) improved nutrition and greater physical activity (lifestyle modifications);
2) metformin and thiazolidinediones (drugs that decrease insulin resistance and glucose production by the liver);
3) acarbose (drug that slows down carbohydrate absorption);
4) orlistat (drug used to control weight gain);
5) possibly inhibitors of the renin-angiotensin system (drugs used for the treatment of high blood pressure, heart failure, and diabetic nephropathy). This class of medication requires further research because benefits were not observed in all the studies;
6) bariatric surgery, or weight-loss surgery, which involves reducing the size of the stomach or inducing malabsorption.

6. What factors are responsible for the development of the complications of diabetes?

In the 1990s, two major studies definitively confirmed that the microvascular complications of diabetes (retinopathy, nephropathy, neuropathy) are primarily related to high blood glucose over several years. The first study, an American-Canadian trial (DCCT) published in 1993, followed 1440 patients with type 1 diabetes. The second, a British trial (UKPDS) published in 1998, followed 4209 patients with type 2 diabetes. Both studies found that diabetes, whether type 1 or type 2, must be aggressively treated and that the complications of diabetes can be prevented by keeping target blood glucose levels as close to normal as possible.

A number of more recent studies have confirmed the importance of optimal blood glucose control to avoid complications, particularly microvascular complications (retinopathy, nephropathy, neuropathy). The STENO-2 study demonstrated that intensive treatment of multiples factors including blood glucose, blood pressure, and cholesterol not only reduced microvascular complications (retinopathy, nephropathy, neuropathy), but also lowered mortality rates and cut the number of cardiovascular events (infarcts, stroke). The study also confirmed the importance of controlling all the risk factors.

Long-term follow-up in the DCCT and STENO-2 studies has shown that the benefits of treatment continue for several years after the intensive treatment.

7. Is it possible to prevent the appearance of complications?

The prevention of complications presents one of the great challenges of research into diabetes. Thanks to our better understanding of the physiopathological mechanisms responsible for the complications of diabetes, there are a few studies now evaluating drugs that may be able to prevent the complications of diabetes, regardless of blood glucose control.

We have already mentioned the major role that high blood glucose levels play in the development of the complications of diabetes. A number of studies have shown that high blood sugar is associated with an overproduction of an enzyme called kinase C, and that this enzyme is involved in the development of the complications. The pharmaceutical industry has developed a kinase C protein inhibitor and demonstrated that this drug can prevent complications in animals with diabetes.

Studies of the effects of kinase C inhibitors on diabetic retinopathy and neuropathy in humans are currently underway. Such drugs could eventually make it possible to prevent complications even when optimal control of blood glucose is difficult. Researchers are also beginning to study drugs inhibiting growth factors that play a role in the development of retinopathy (pegaptanib, ranibizumab and bevacizumab).

8. Is it easy to control diabetes?

DCCT and UKPDS studies have shown that it is difficult to reach normal blood glucose levels. In Canada, the DICE study looked at patients followed by front-line doctors and revealed that close to 50% of people with type 2 diabetes did not attain their recommended treatment targets. Making this task easier depends not only on using the medications that already exist, but also looking for new treatments.

9. **How is it possible to prevent a gradual deterioration of glycemic control over time?**

   Interventions to preserve the function of the pancreatic beta cells and a residual secretion of insulin are also important topics of research at the moment. In animals, thiazolidinedione and incretin drugs have been shown to have a positive effect on the beta cells by decreasing cell death and increasing cell proliferation.

10. **What is new in the treatment of diabetes?**

    A number of antidiabetic drugs and new techniques are currently being studied or will soon be available in Canada. The following are worth noting:

    1) drugs that slow gastric emptying, giving time to the pancreas to react, such as pramlintide (Symlin®);

    2) drugs that slow gastric emptying simulate the secretion of insulin by the pancreas (in response to elevated blood sugar) and decrease the production of glucagon (a hormone that blocks the effect of insulin and increases blood sugar). Such drugs include GLP-1 analogs (incretin drugs) such as exenatide (Byetta®) and liraglutide. These drugs are administered subcutaneously, although a form that will be delivered intranasally is currently in development. These drugs also have a positive side effect, as they induce weight loss;

    3) new ways of administering insulin; Oralin®, for example, is delivered orally and absorbed through the mucous membranes of the mouth;

    4) inhibitors of glucose transport in the kidney that increase the elimination of glucose through the urine, such as sergliflozin and dapagliflozin;

    5) new technical procedures to connect an insulin pump to a continuous blood glucose monitor, to create a kind of artificial pancreas.

11. **What are the challenges of transplants?**

    o **Pancreas transplants** have been successfully executed in various Canadian hospitals, including the CHUM Notre-Dame Hospital. The two major obstacles to pancreas transplants are the shortage of donors and the side effects of anti-rejection drugs.

o   More recently, there has been progress made in the transplants of **islets of Langerhans**, which involve the injection insulin-making pancreatic cells. An innovative group of researchers from Edmonton, Alberta have improved the technique of isolating the islets of Langerhans and used new combinations of anti-rejection drugs (without cortisone). These transplants are performed under local anesthesia on ambulatory patients. A catheter is inserted into the portal vein entering the liver and the islets are injected with a syringe, after which the patient goes home. One of the difficulties encountered is the fact that the isolation technique enables the recovery of only 20% of the islets. Therefore, two and sometimes three donor pancreases are required to obtain a sufficient amount of islets of Langerhans for the transplant. In addition, the destruction of the islets over time means that the cure offered by this technique is temporary. The problem of donor shortage is therefore all the more acute. Improved techniques for isolating the islets, however, should provide a partial solution to this problem.

o   New avenues are also being explored with the goal of finding insulin-producing and secreting cells for transplant. **Genetic engineering** now enables us to take cells from the intestine or liver and genetically program them to produce insulin. These specialized cells respond to changes in blood glucose: an increase in blood glucose increases the production and secretion of the hormone, and a decrease in blood glucose decreases the production and secretion of the hormone. If these cells are genetically reprogrammed to produce insulin, they are stimulated by hyperglycemia and inhibited by a lowering of blood glucose. Researchers have demonstrated that this is effective in mice and can cure diabetes in animals—even without anti-rejection drugs. There remains a lot of work to do before this technique can be used on human, of course, but it is all within the realm of the possible!

o   Over the past few years, there has been a great deal of discussion about embryonic stem cells and stem cells from adult human bone marrow. These stem cells have the innate capacity to become any type of mature cell, including insulin-producing pancreatic cells. Experiments in this area have only just begun, but they have been very encouraging.

12. What benefits can diabetes research bring?

It is clear that diabetes represents an immense challenge due to the rapidly increasing frequency of the disease, caused primarily by the aging of the population and the ever-rising number of people who are overweight. Research, however, has brought us new pharmacological and technological advances that can not only control blood glucose but , maybe one day, actually cure the disease and its complications.

Research into diabetes, which involves participation of a number of Canadian researchers, is being carried out all over the world and continues to bring a great deal of hope to people with diabetes.

Diabetes Follow-up Tools

1. **How is diabetes "managed"?**

   Managing diabetes presents a number of challenges. Medical follow-ups, blood glucose self-monitoring, diet, exercise and medication are all important aspects of treatment that people with diabetes have to keep in mind at all times.

   It can all seem overwhelming. Diabetes requires people to reconsider their entire lifestyle and make a long-term commitment to managing the condition. Therefore, the easiest way to improve treatment is to take things one step at a time instead of trying to change every habit at once. People should set clear and realistic goals, **congratulate themselves for each goal successfully achieved, and learn from any difficulties they encounter.**

2. **Are there any tools to help with diabetes follow-up?**

   People with diabetes have several tools available to help them follow up on their disease. A self-monitoring logbook is obviously essential. Another useful tool is a "journal of personal goals", which should list the goals of the person with diabetes as they relate to five important aspects of the follow-up: medical follow-up, care, diet, medication and well-being. People are advised to select any number of these objectives and rank them in order of priority (for example, from 1 to 5).

   It is a good idea to consult this journal from time to time. Checking it periodically can help keep track of progress, understand why some goals are more difficult to reach, determine the means to reach them, or set new objectives. (*See the Model journal on pages 279 to 281.*)

3. Is there a tool to help manage diet?

A meal plan drawn up with the aid of a dietician is an essential tool for people with diabetes.

4. Which tests and targets help achieve optimal control of diabetes?

Medical follow-up of a person with diabetes includes various tests, including tests for blood glucose, glycosylated hemoglobin (A1C), lipid profile and blood pressure. Remember that glycosylated hemoglobin is used to determine how the blood sugar has been controlled over the last three months.

Target values for the various tests or measurements are presented in the "Targets for optimal control" chart on page 282.

5. How are the test results used?

Test results enable a doctor to choose the appropriate treatment for a person with diabetes, to assess its effectiveness, and to make the necessary adjustments. The "Test follow-up journal" (*see page 283*) can be used to keep track of relevant information, including test results. These results enable a person with diabetes to follow the treatment as it evolves and discuss it with the doctor. They can even be used as a motivational tool.

JOURNAL OF PERSONAL GOALS

What follows is a list of goals relevant to a person with diabetes. Choose the ones that are most important to you (a maximum of 5) and number them according to their priority. Revise the objectives you have chosen periodically.

DATES					
MEDICAL FOLLOW-UP					
See the doctor at least twice a year					
Inquire about the results of tests and examinations					
Check blood pressure regularly					
Check microalbuminuria once a year					
See the opthalmologist regularly, as recommended					
CARE AND RECOMMENDATIONS					
Enter blood glucose levels in my self-monitoring logbook and analyze them as advised					
In case of illness, check blood glucose levels more often					
Compare readings from the glucose meter with a blood test at least once a year					
Keep carbohydrates within reach at all times (at least two portions of 15 g each)					
Examine my feet every day					
Do not smoke					
Do physical activity regularly (everyday if possible)					
Wear a diabetic ID bracelet or pendant					

DATES					
Inform driving authorities (in Quebec, the Société d'assurance automobile du Québec (SAAQ))					
DIET					
Eat the recommended amount of carbohydrates at each meal					
Eat balanced meals (carbohydrates, proteins, fats)					
Choose fibre-rich foods					
Have evening snacks, as recommended					
Keep regular mealtimes					
Measure food portions from time to time					
Keep a regular food journal					
Eat only fats that are recommended					
Drink alcohol only with food					
MEDICATION					
Take medications as prescribed by the doctor					
Know the names of my antidiabetic drugs					
Enter all the antidiabetic drugs I take and any changes of dosage in the self-monitoring logbook					
Keep a complete and up-to-date list of all drugs (names, doses) and bring it to all medical appointments					
Follow the insulin adjustment rules					
Know the best times to take the drugs					

DATES					
Know how to manage skipped doses of antidiabetic drugs					
Make sure that any antidiabetic drugs or natural health products do not worsen my condition					
WELL-BEING					
Identify stress factors with the most effect					
Improve my reaction to stress					
Set aside at least 10 minutes a day for relaxation					
Speak to my support network about my diabetes					
Manage my time in a way that meets my needs					
MY PERSONAL GOALS					

Signature: _____

TARGETS FOR OPTIMAL CONTROL

Glucose	
Glycosylated hemoglobin (A1C)	≤ 0.070 or 7%
Fasting or pre-meal blood glucose	4 mmol/L – 7 mmol/L
Blood glucose 2 hours after beginning of meals	5 mmol/L – 10 mmol/L (Individualize: 5 mmol/L to 8 mmol/L if A1C > 0.070 or 7%)
Lipid Profile	
Triglycerides	< 1.5 mmol/L
LDL Cholesterol	≤ 2.0 mmol/L
Total cholesterol / HDL Cholesterol	< 4
Kidneys	
Albumin/creatinine ratio	M: < 2.0 mg/mmol; W: < 2.8 mg/mmol
Microalbuminuria	< 20 µg/min or < 30 mg/day
Others	
Blood pressure	≤ 130/80 mm Hg
Normal weight	< 65 years old: BMI* 18.5 – 24.9 ≥ 65 years old: BMI 18.6 – 29.9
Waist	M: < 102 cm; W: < 88 cm

* BMI: body mass index (weight in kg/height in m²)
≤ : less than or equal
≥ : more than or equal
< : less than
> : more than

Name: _____

Date						
Weight (kg)						
Height (m)						
BMI (kg/m²)						
Waist circumference (cm)						
Blood pressure (≤ 130/80 mm Hg)						
Blood glucose (blood test) Before meal: 4 mmol/L – 7 mmol/L						
After meal: 5 mmol/L – 10 mmol/L (Individualize : 5 mmol/L to 8 mmol/L if A1C > 0.070 or 7%)						
Glycosylated hemoglobin (A1C) (≤ 0.070)						
Triglycerides (< 1.5 mmol/L)						
LDL Cholesterol (≤ 2.0 mmol/L)						
HDL Cholesterol M ≥ 1.0 mmol/L W ≥ 1.3 mmol/L						
Total cholesterol / HDL Cholesterol (< 4)						
Albumin: creatinin ratio M < 2.0 mg/mmol W < 2.8 mg/mmol)						
Microalbuminuria (< 20 µg/min ou < 30 mg/day)						
Creatinine clearance (>1.5 mL/s)						

Annexe

BLOOD GLUCOSE CONVERSION CHART

mmol/L*	mg/dL**	mmol/L	mg/dL
1.4	25	11.2	202
1.6	29	11.6	209
1.8	32	12.0	216
2.0	36	12.4	223
2.4	43	12.8	230
2.8	50	13.2	238
3.2	58	13.6	245
3.6	65	14.0	252
4.0	72	14.4	259
4.4	79	14.8	266
4.8	86	15.2	274
5.2	94	15.6	281
5.6	101	16.0	288
6.0	108	16.4	295
6.4	115	16.8	302
6.8	122	17.2	309
7.0	126	17.6	317
7.2	130	18.0	324
7.6	137	18.5	333
8.0	144	19.0	342
8.4	151	19.5	351
8.8	158	20.0	360
9.2	166	20.5	369
9.6	173	21.0	378
10.0	180	21.5	387
10.4	187	22.0	396
10.8	194	22.5	405

Target values before meals and at bedtime (values 4.0–7.0 mmol/L / 72–126 mg/dL)

*   mmol/L x 18 = mg/dL

** mg/dL ÷ 18 = mmol/L